The New Friendly Islanders

Also by the same author:

Royal Visit to Tonga (Pitkin, 1954)
The Friendly Islanders (Hodder & Stoughton, 1967)
A Guide to Pitcairn (Ed.) (British South Pacific Office, Fiji, 1970)
Treason at Ten: Fiji at the Crossroads (Hodder & Stoughton, 1989)

The New Friendly Islanders

The Tonga of King Taufa'ahau Tupou IV

KENNETH BAIN

Published to mark the occasion of the
seventy-fifth birthday of the King on 4 July 1993

Hodder & Stoughton

LONDON SYDNEY AUCKLAND

British Library Cataloguing in Publication Data

Bain, Kenneth
  The New Friendly Islanders.
  I. Title
  813[F]

  ISBN 0-340-58338-X

Published by Hodder and Stoughton,
a division of Hodder and Stoughton Ltd,
Mill Road, Dunton Green, Sevenoaks, Kent TN13 2YA.
Editorial Office: 47 Bedford Square, London WCIB 3DP.

Photoset by Rowland Phototypesetting Ltd,
Bury St Edmunds, Suffolk

Printed in Great Britain by
St Edmundsbury Press Ltd, Bury St Edmunds, Suffolk

For Siale Vuki, Anga'aefonu, Melino Lavulo
and
Sophia 'Atu-o-hakautapu,
all of whom are among the inheritors of
THE NEW FRIENDLY ISLANDERS

Contents

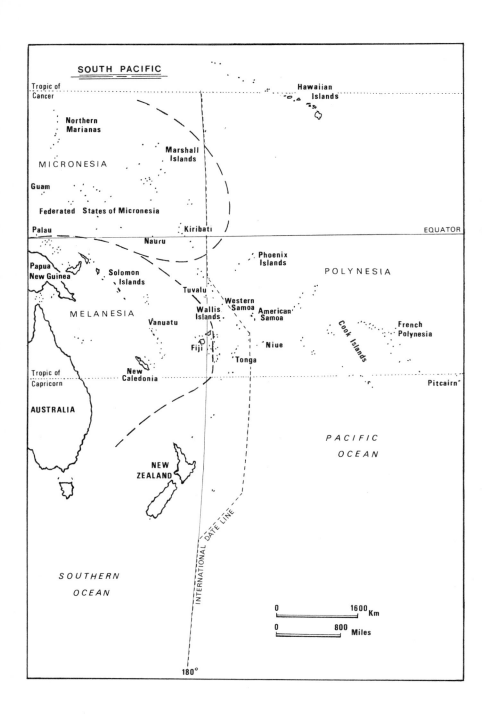

SOUTH PACIFIC

Tropic of Cancer

Hawaiian Islands

Northern Marianas

Marshall Islands

MICRONESIA

Guam

Federated States of Micronesia

Palau

EQUATOR

Kiribatı

Nauru

Phoenix Islands

POLYNESIA

Papua New Guinea

Solomon Islands

Tuvalu

Western Samoa

American Samoa

MELANESIA

Vanuatu

Wallis Islands

French Polynesia

Cook Islands

Fiji

Niue

Tonga

Tropic of Capricorn

New Caledonia

Pitcairn

AUSTRALIA

PACIFIC OCEAN

NEW ZEALAND

INTERNATIONAL DATE LINE

SOUTHERN OCEAN

0   1600 Km

0   800 Miles

180°

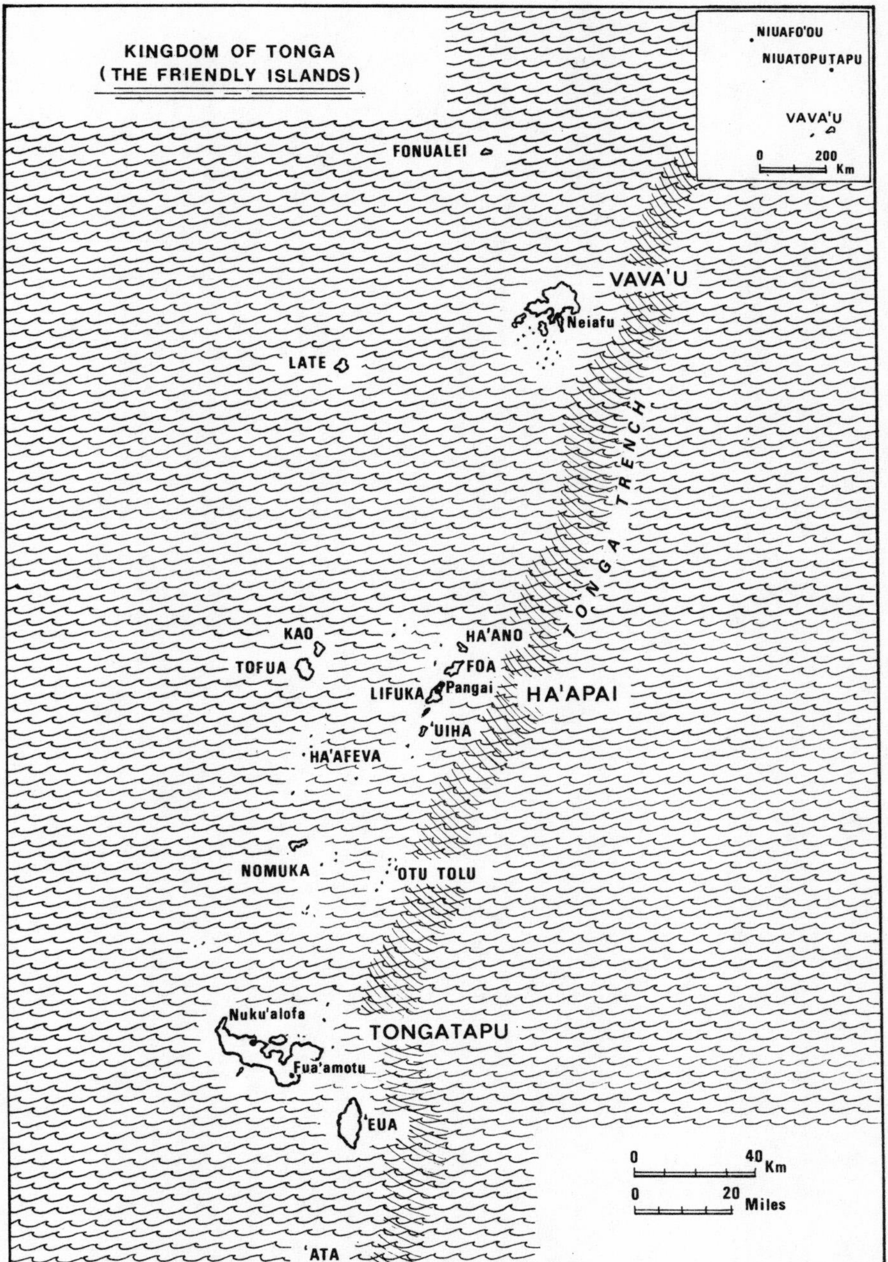

KINGDOM OF TONGA
(THE FRIENDLY ISLANDS)

NIUAFO'OU
NIUATOPUTAPU

VAVA'U

0   200
         Km

FONUALEI

VAVA'U
Neiafu

LATE

TONGA TRENCH

KAO   HA'ANO
TOFUA   FOA
        LIFUKA Pangai   HA'APAI
        'UIHA
HA'AFEVA

NOMUKA   'OTU TOLU

Nuku'alofa
        TONGATAPU
    Fua'amotu

'EUA

0   40
              Km
0   20
         Miles

'ATA

Foreword

In my Foreword to *The Friendly Islanders* in July 1966, I referred to the many changes in Tonga in the years since Kenneth Bain served as Secretary to the Government in the fifties. In that book, he described contemporary Tonga as a study of custom in transition. If these judgments were accurate then, they are even more relevant today since the pace is faster. Our great globe has shrunk; distances are no longer what they were; and the staggering technological accomplishments of the latter years of the twentieth century have brought us all to recognition and membership of one world to share – or to imperil.

The human race now has greater opportunities than ever before; but there are also far greater risks. For small island states such as Tonga, with a precarious economic base, this is especially true. We may not be able to exercise fundamental influence over great human issues or decisions; but, like every other country and people, we stand to gain or lose, progress or stagnate, by the nature of those decisions and our capacity to respond to them. That our life is no longer a matter of 'waiting for the coconuts to fall' is demonstrated not least by the many Tongans who have achieved so much in the United States, Australia, New Zealand, Britain and elsewhere.

We in Tonga are thus not immune to the forces at work in the world beyond our Pacific island shores; but we must continue to be critically vigilant about what we embrace and what we should reject if the essentials of our culture, language and institutions, both spiritual and temporal, are to endure.

In his third book about us, Kenneth Bain has again been a close observer looking in from outside. His new, at times controversial, perceptions of Tonga and Tongans, largely through Tongans themselves, are written with insight, frankness and humour. They will interest two quite different groups of readers: those who are Tongan and who are gently nudged 'to see ourselves as others see us'; and those non-Tongans who seek to penetrate the apparent mysteries of our culture and to understand its virtues and weaknesses, and why we think and act as we do.

This timely book may also serve to reinforce the need in our society for tolerance and acceptance of economic innovation and structured change. Without this, we will not remain true to our heritage or be equipped to meet the challenges of the twenty-first century. Whatever else happens in the decades that lie ahead, it is my deepest wish, my vision, that all of us will continue to be proud to say, truthfully and honestly, that Tonga is still Tonga.

TAUFA'AHAU TUPOU

4 July, 1992
The Palace,
Nuku'alofa,
TONGA

List of Illustrations

The Tongans

Defence Force and captain of a naval patrol vessel. His wife is Nanasi, daughter of Baron Vaea and Tuputupu.

Havea Tu'iha'ateiho, a noble. Former Deputy Premier. Deceased.

'Ulukalala Ata, a noble. Former Minister of Police and Prisons. The 'old' 'Ulukalala. Deceased.

Viliami Fukofuka, Representative of the People in the Legislative Assembly.

Part Two

'Eseta Fusitu'a, Public Relations and Information Officer, Prime Minister's Office in 1991. Now Deputy Chief Secretary and Deputy Secretary to Cabinet.

'Inoke Faletau, Director of the Commonwealth Foundation, erstwhile High Commissioner for Tonga in London.

Fusitu'a, a noble. Speaker of the Legislative Assembly.

Kalaniuvalu, a noble.

Viela 'Ileini Tupou, Principal Assistant Secretary, Ministry of Foreign Affairs.

Dr 'Ana Maui Taufe'ulungaki, a Deputy Director of Education.

Futa Helu, Director of 'Atenisi Institute.

Masina Tu'i'onetoa, Assistant Secretary, Office of the Governor of Vava'u.

Tu'i'afitu, a noble. Governor of Vava'u.

Mikio Filitonga, owner of the Vava'u Guest House.

Viliami 'Afeaki, Representative of the People in the Legislative Assembly.

Papiloa Foliaki, owner of the Friendly Islander motel. Erstwhile Representative of the People in the Legislative Assembly.

'Ila, Friendly Islander motel employee.

Bishop Patelesio Finau, Roman Catholic Bishop of Tonga and Niue.

Loka Mafi, head of the Philatelic Bureau in 1991. Deceased.

Pesi Fonua, journalist. Editor and publisher of the magazine *Matangi Tonga*.

Rev. 'Amanaki Havea, lately head of the Free Wesleyan Church of Tonga.

'Akilisi Pohiva, Representative of the People in the Legislative Assembly.

Hale Vete, retired businessman.

Dr Langi Kavaliku, Deputy Prime Minister since September 1991 and Minister for Education, Works and Civil Aviation.

Mana Latu, a Deputy Director of Education.

Dr Tilitili Puloka, Royal Physician.

'Alone, an official chauffeur.

Mekita Pale, Acting Chief Inspector of Police. The Queen's Security Officer.

David Tupou, Attorney General and Minister for Justice.

Dr 'Alokihakau 'Eva, former surgeon. Deceased.

Sione Kité, High Commissioner for Tonga in London from May 1992.

Together with the many young men and women in whose hands the future of Tonga may well rest.

PART ONE

What is the future if there is no past?

Eileen Nancy Greville

1

The Unpacific Pacific

The South Pacific has become a nervously unsettled part of the globe. It is no good pretending, as some do, that it is otherwise. Two military coups in Fiji in 1987 sent shockwaves to every island government. There have been constitutional crises, strikes, riots and/or bloodshed in Vanuatu, New Caledonia, French Polynesia and Papua New Guinea (where there was attempted secession and nearly civil war as well). They will not be the last such occurrences. Notwithstanding the huge ocean distances between tiny pinpoints of land, all are affected in one way or another by events in neighbouring islands and beyond.

A great oceanic triangle in the Central and South Pacific embraces three distinct racial, linguistic and cultural groupings: Melanesia to the west, Micronesia to the north and Polynesia to the east. The Maoris of New Zealand represent the southernmost penetration of Polynesia; Hawaii the most northern; and Pitcairn and Easter Island the eastern extremities. Fiji is the crossroads of Melanesia and Polynesia. To the west lie New Caledonia, Vanuatu, the Solomon Islands and Papua New Guinea, all of whose people are black skinned, fuzzy haired and stocky. The Micronesians to the north – Nauru, Kiribati, the Marshall Islands, the Federated States of Micronesia, Palau and Guam – are pale skinned and more spare in build. They are atoll dwellers. Their faces carry visible characteristics of the Philippines and Indonesia. To the east of Fiji lie the two Samoas, Western and American, the Cook Islands, French Polynesia, Niue and the last surviving monarchy in Polynesia, the Kingdom of Tonga.

Suddenly it seems that the world is on the doorstep of almost every island capital. The mini-states – independent politically but dependent economically – are the latest playground for big power politics, entrepreneurial adventurism and cheque-book diplomacy, whatever some governments may allege to the contrary. Custom and tradition survive precariously in a region of universal Christian influence and apparent unity, yet with deep sectarian rivalry and fragmentation. Emigration queues and visitors' visa applications at resident metropolitan missions seem never-ending.

Amid all this, the Kingdom of Tonga outwardly remains a

steadfast anachronism. Its monarchy and royal family seem not just to be intact but to be energetically expanding their sphere of influence.

The constitution is semi-feudal and grandly Victorian. Full parliamentary democracy does not exist. Oligarchy, however, does: an oligarchy of the royal family and the nobility. It is the sovereign's prerogative to appoint the prime minister and other ministers; but not on the basis of electoral endorsement or parliamentary support. They retain their offices during the sovereign's pleasure. Which may seem to mean for life, or nearly so. Thus Queen Salote appointed her first son as Premier in 1949; and he, as King, similarly installed his younger brother in 1965. So two royal princely brothers successively headed the Government for forty-two years from 1949 to 1991.

Institutionally conservative though it may be, Tonga has flung open its doors to tourism and thus the wider influences of the outside world, good and bad. Except on Sundays when, for example, no aircraft movements are permitted and the churches are full. The country's apparent stability is seen as an investment attraction, yet there are the usual murmurings of corruption in high places. The public perception is that the King and Crown Prince openly dabble in business enterprises. Similarly, the only royal daughter, Princess Pilolevu, who resided in London as wife of the Tonga High Commissioner from 1989 to 1992. The Crown Prince – articulate, urbane, polished and linguistically versatile – has not married; and the consequent apparent lack of secure direct succession is a worry not only to the King and Queen but to many conservative Tongans. It is a more complicating factor than it may seem.

The developmental and technological advances in the King's twenty-seven-year reign are remarkable: over fifty aircraft movements in a six-day week, instead of one ship a month; international direct dial fax and telephone; a virile press in Tongan and English; taped television; FM/AM broadcasting and satellite dishes. It is a long way from the village criers who only forty years ago passed out oral instructions to the people without the aid of radio or newspapers.

Potential aid donors pour in from metropolitan governments and international agencies. They, with the carpetbaggers and the commercially dubious, seek to pay homage at the Palace; ministerial offices and select island resorts draw them as moths to a candle. A royal connection was never more courted; royal patronage never more prized; and, some would contend, never more available. In a burgeoning budget, foreign aid funds have spawned valium-like developmental dependence.

Discontent and pressure for constitutional and structural change in parliament, government and society is no longer concealed beneath the surface of life in contemporary Tonga. They have now found voice, in private and in public. In other ways – through investment enterprise, the creation of wealth by a new monied middle class and a widening economic gap between patrician and plebeian – the tempo of change in the past decade has been fast, inexorable and sustained. Not so in the institutions and machinery of government. That is where the momentum ends – in the doldrums of frustration for the poor and the less privileged.

As one recent commentator arguably concluded: 'It would not be surprising if Tonga became the next nation for political unrest in the South Pacific.' He confessed his research was limited to library sources, interviews and observations during a week in Tonga in March 1988. This was too close for comfort perhaps to the cataclysmic events four hundred miles away in Fiji a few months earlier.

Plus ça change; plus ce n'est pas la même chose. In this case, that is. A great reservoir of vibrant youthful energy, not least among young women, cries out for productive opportunity in its island home or beyond. The wealth of future human resources is there waiting for leadership and inspirational guidance. From within.

2

In the Beginning . . .

In the dim far-distant days of the past, Tongamatamoana was the great god of the heavens and his only daughter lived as one of the earthly creatures below. As the god's daughter grew to womanhood, she became as beautiful as any star in the universe; and to preserve her from earthly danger, Tongamatamoana took her away from the earth to the sky where she could enjoy his protection. So that the risk of earthly intrusion should be slight, the great god made to his house a hazardous pathway and few there were with knowledge of its beginning.

When her friends of the earth came to know that the girl had vanished, they searched in every village in every land. But they could find no trace of her. Then it was that the priests said that she had returned to the sky, since she was of the gods and not of worldly men. The young men of the villages sought to find and traverse the path to the heavens to bring back the beautiful maiden they had lost. None succeeded; for all who made the attempt died on the way and did not return, and no one could find the reason.

At last there were but two left who would make the attempt: the fishermen brothers, Maui Kisikisi and Maui 'Atalanga. Together they set out to face the wrath of the god and make their way to the girl's heavenly home. When they had found the place at which the path began, their way was easy until they passed Pulotu, where the spirits of the chiefly dead leave this world for the spirit world beyond. Soon they were bewildered and lost and unable to perceive which way to continue.

Maui 'Atalanga said, 'Let us stay here awhile so that we may find someone who will be able to tell us which way we should take; for I fear that if we do not do so, we may meet our death as have our brothers before us.'

So Maui Kisikisi and Maui 'Atalanga waited by the side of the path and, as the day drew to its close, they saw in the distance the figure of a woman coming towards them. Observing that she was a goddess, the two brothers, though in great fear, resolved to speak to her. 'O great one of the sky, is this the way which leads to the home of Tongamatamoana and his daughter?' they asked.

'Yes,' the woman replied, 'the path lies ahead.'

'But how may we reach the heavens?' they asked. 'For we have heard that many have died on the way.'

'If you have good heart and take heed of what I tell you,' said the goddess, 'you will be safe and will find what you seek. If you do not, then you too will die and the daughter of Tongamatamoana will forever remain beyond the sight of earthly men.'

'Pray tell us,' they beseeched her, 'and we shall obey.'

'Then follow me,' said the woman, 'and do as I say.'

So they started on their journey once more. After they had been walking for many hours and were growing cold and hungry, the woman turned to them and said, 'A short distance from this place you will find the most succulent food set on the wayside. Since I can read what is in your minds and in your hearts, I know that you are nearly dead from hunger, for you have not eaten for many hours. But should you touch or eat anything, you will die and your spirits will wander for ever in the torment of the underworld below Pulotu. If you can resist the temptation to eat, you will live to continue your journey.'

Presently the two brothers began to smell the aromas of roast pig and fish of the sea and fowls of the air. As they turned a corner they saw row upon row of choice delicacies set on banana leaves at the edge of the path. Although they were exhausted from hunger and in great distress, they determined to obey the words of the goddess and to walk past the food. Then Maui 'Atalanga stopped and made move to taste it, his patience and strength at an end; but Maui Kisikisi put out a hand to his brother and drew him away. Together they went on their journey, their hunger unsatisfied.

In a while, they forgot their hunger and once again ahead of them they saw the goddess waiting and smiling at them.

'Well done,' she said, 'you have proved yourselves worthy to continue your quest.'

When they had gone a little further, the way suddenly narrowed into a hollow tunnel so tiny that they could not pass through it. 'Do not be alarmed,' said their companion, 'if I strike you; for I must now change you from your human shape into something smaller.'

With that, she hit them both on the head. At once they were changed into cats and so could pass through the tunnel. Then the path became still narrower. Once again the goddess struck them on the head. They were changed into rats and so could make their way through the opening. Although in great fear that they would never return to their earthly bodies, the two brothers found the courage to continue their journey and were astonished to find the path becoming wide again. No longer were they cats or rats, but men.

Soon they entered a village of fine houses, green grass and trees.

'You have done well,' said their companion. 'There is the house for which you are searching.' And with that she left them and was not seen again.

Overjoyed at their good fortune, Maui Kisikisi and Maui 'Atalanga approached the house of Tongamatamoana and were greeted by the girl for whom they had come.

'You are welcome in my father's house,' she said, 'for the heavenly path is hard and narrow and many there are who have failed on the way.'

When they had been given food and water, Maui Kisikisi explained a second purpose of their journey: to acquire a fish hook with the power to draw up land from the ocean, for they had heard that the great god Tongamatamoana was the possessor of such hooks.

'When my father comes back,' said the girl, 'you may tell him what you seek. He will invite you to examine his fish hooks and may even offer you whichever one you choose. I advise you to ignore the many fine hooks in his collection and to ask him for a small rusty hook which you will see together with the others. Even though it looks weak and old, it is this hook alone which has the strength to do what you want.'

Tongamatamoana returned to the house to eat and after he had satisfied his hunger the two brothers placed their request before him. They explained that the worldly place in which they lived was now too small for the many people who dwelt there and more land was needed. When they had finished, the god and the brothers went to look at Tongamatamoana's collection of fish hooks. At once they saw what his daughter had told them was true. There among many fine shining hooks was one which was rusted and dirty. Trusting the words of the girl, they asked the god if they might have it.

'Very well,' said Tongamatamoana, 'you shall have this hook, for I have heard of your courage in finding your way here and I believe you both to be brave and honest. Although it looks so poor, this is a sacred hook which is not to be given to ordinary men. Go now; and when you draw up the first land from the bottomless depths of the ocean with this hook, you shall call it Tongatapu, or sacred Tonga.'

So Maui Kisikisi and Maui 'Atalanga returned to the earth and one day, as they fished in the waters of the ocean with the sacred hook granted to them by the great god of the sky, they pulled up the

28

island of Tongatapu from the bottom of the sea. Then they went further and drew up Ha'apai and Vava'u and other small islands, all of which together they called Tonga after the god who had endowed the earth with this new and blessed land.

The old fish hook was given the name *Tonga Fusifonua* which means the hook that pulled up the land of Tonga.

And that is how the islands of Tonga arose from the ocean as part of the earth world . . .

All these islands (and there are some 150 of them) lie within that great Polynesian belt in the South Pacific Ocean. The three main groups – Tongatapu in the south, Ha'apai in the centre and Vava'u in the north – cover an area of 270 square miles between 18° and 20° south of the equator. There are two groups of islands, distinct in character: the western line is volcanic and hilly, the eastern coralline and flat. Together they support today a modest population of about 100,000.

Running east of north from New Zealand lies the great Tonga Trench. Formed when a dense oceanic crust slips below a lighter oceanic crust or continental ledge, such trenches or rifts plunge down into unimaginable subterranean depths. East of the island of 'Ata, the Tonga Trench penetrates 10,800 metres (35,433 feet) below the surface of the South Pacific Ocean. It is second only to the Mariana Trench in Micronesia as the earth's deepest. The difference is a mere 124 metres (407 feet).

So the bottom of the nearby ocean from which Maui 'Atalanga and Maui Kisikisi fished up those islands of Tonga plumbs a depth that is 2,000 metres greater than the height of Mount Everest.

It must have been some fish hook.

3

Veni Vidi *but not* Vici

February 1991

Have you ever gone back, years later, to see and hopefully to revive an old love – a city, a house, a beach, a girl, a holiday, an early movie? If you have, you will know that retrospective curiosity is an unreliable guide to latter-day fulfilment. As no one remains the same, neither does a country, however ocean-girt and geographically remote. Nothing is as it was. The dream is not the reality. Nostalgic glow is best with after-dinner cognac; then it has a mirage-like mesmerism.

But only then. There are few dreams and fewer illusions that survive for long in the real world. They are endangered species, like our assumptions of how life was before urban decay, inflation, heroin, high-street muggings, racial confrontation, Aids, international terrorism, computer crime, cable TV, mass tourism and plastic card credit. Was it ever otherwise? Memory is most often kind and forgiving, or so it is adumbrated by those who perceive nostalgia as a trap for the unwary.

Yet here I am, about to return – after thirty-five years and but two fleeting day visits – to rediscover, and thus to compare and reappraise, a small South Pacific island nation and its people. Maybe it is an arrogance to attempt. It won't work, some would say, because the ball-game has changed and the goal-posts have shifted. The past reveals nothing. The future can take care of itself. Buy now, pay later. The present is all.

Or is it? Well, we shall see. Hopefully in this case, it will prove better to arrive than to travel. It was certainly so the first time round.

July 1953

. . . The voyage had been mercifully short – only thirty-six hours from Suva to Nuku'alofa after one of those frantic surges through aerial space from London. The wartime freighter *Waikawa* fell somewhat below the luxury class of shipboard travel. There were eight passengers all of whom – apart from myself – had embarked

in Sydney and were bound for Vancouver. The only hoped-for
relief from the tedium of each other's company during the ship's
wallowing progress across the Pacific was the prospect of Bastille
Day in Tahiti. Strong and regular pressure was applied to the
ship's officers to ensure the success of the delaying tactics which
were essential in Nuku'alofa if the ship were not to arrive and
depart from the harbour of Papeete before the excitements began
there . . .

. . . An hour out from Tongatapu, we seemed to be in mid-
ocean. Then a flat smudge of coconut palms began to grow out
of the sea. Soon this was surmounted in part by a line of stately
Norfolk pines flanking the sea shore. Through the leaves and
branches glinted the white walls of Queen Salote's Palace and
Royal Chapel. The Tongan Royal Standard floated from the Palace
tower. Further along the shore, the Union Flag marked the British
Residency. I was about to transfer for three years from British
Colonial Service via Canadian to Tongan articles . . .

I was twenty-nine. On loan from the colonial Government of Fiji as
Secretary to the Government of Tonga. It sounded great, but my
education was just beginning.

'Up till now,' said a benign Colonial Secretary, gazing at me
from behind deep horn-rimmed spectacles, 'you have seen matters of
policy from only one Secretariat perspective – the bottom of the
assistant secretary ladder.'

'Yes, sir. I'm afraid so,' I replied weakly.

'Ever had anyone working to you before?'

'No. Actually I haven't.'

'Well then. Things are going to be different for you in Tonga.
You'll have to learn some new tricks.'

Only too true, as it turned out – and not only in that way. The
official road ahead proved to be complex, tortuous and bewildering.
Nothing was ever what it seemed. The unbelievable perforce became
the believable. Because it was so. There was a new language – and
a new psychology – to learn.

The first file I opened contained an appeal to the Cabinet by a
prisons sergeant. The Minister for Prisons had suspended him for
alleged misconduct (i.e. being disrespectful) towards the said minister. What authority had the Cabinet in the matter? The Prisons Regulations were silent. Except that there was provision for appeal in such
cases to the Minister of Police. Why hadn't the Minister considered

the appeal, since the sergeant had already been under suspension for about six months? Without pay.

My God, I thought, this is terrible – and said so to the official interpreter, who chose that moment to venture into my office for the first time.

'Yes, it certainly is,' he said fervently. 'Something must be done. But I would suggest that you put it to Cabinet first. That's our normal procedure. The Minister will wish to have the authority of Cabinet to enable him to proceed.'

'Whatever for? The regulations are clear.'

He did not reply. He had given his advice.

I studied the files. On the basis of past practice, the interpreter was right. And from then on, ministerial memoranda from the police would present a problem, suggest no solution, make no recommendation and invariably end with 'For Cabinet consideration': on one occasion in respect of a bicycle allowance for a new messenger.

So I did on Day One what I was advised to do, drawing the attention of Ministers of the Tongan Crown to the enormity of the delay and the palpable grievance of the appellant. Then I discovered independently that the interpreter happened to be the brother of the suspended sergeant. It was the interpreter who had placed the 'Immediate' tag on my first file. He confessed to the relationship when asked, but had not thought it necessary to divulge it in the first place.

The Cabinet duly instructed the Minister of Police to hear the appeal. He did so – and turned it down. A week later, in the process of relating ministerial responsibilities to the complexities of unfamiliar Tongan chiefly names, I made an interesting discovery: the Minister of Police was also the Minister of Prisons and had thus solemnly heard – and rejected – an appeal against his own decision.

'No, no, no,' the Minister said when, recklessly, I remonstrated with him; while the suspended sergeant continued to languish, workless and unpaid. 'You *papalangi*s don't understand the Tongan way. I heard the appeal as Minister of Police, not as Minister for Prisons. They are two quite different responsibilities under the Law. You must be able to see that.'

Moral and first lesson I said to myself: don't start off by questioning a Tongan Minister – especially when he has combined responsibility for both police and prisons. And remember that truth is relative, not absolute. Polynesian truth anyway.

Veni Vidi *but not* Vici

December 1965

My second arrival in Tonga was a melancholy occasion: that of the death and funeral of the much-loved Queen Salote Tupou III, twelve years later. I was Secretary for Social Services in Fiji at the time.

. . . Half-past three at the RNZAF jetty, the ADC had said. Awake at two-forty-five: shave, shower, black suit, black tie, socks, shoes. Away from the house at three-twenty, the wreath from four former Secretaries to the Government of Tonga enveloped in polythene and resting on the back seat of the car.

One of the last operational Sunderland flying-boats was tied up to the pier as we arrived. Dim figures carried stores, suitcases and uniforms in plastic bags down the steps into the chill steel of the aircraft. One after another we assembled, unspeaking. The Commander of the Fiji Military Forces, the American Consul in Fiji representing the Government, the Australian Commissioner, similarly responsible, the Colonial Secretary, and a one-time Queen's Chaplain and historian of Tonga. Then the Governor of Fiji arrived in the whirl of a Government House car. 'Good trip, Sir,' said the Officer Commanding, as they clambered aboard in the darkness. A roar, and we were off in the blindness of the sea, bumping into the swell inside the reef.

We began to taxi in circular sweeps. 'Sorry about the delay. A bit of compass trouble,' a harassed Flight Sergeant announced. 'How would you like your eggs, Your Excellency?' . . .

During the last hour, we flew into rain squalls below a patchy layer of cloud.

'Why,' I asked the pilot, 'do we not fly above all this at five or six thousand feet?'

He smiled. 'Do you want to freeze the toes off your Governor before he reaches Nuku'alofa? We don't have any heating. The shell of the old crate is paper-thin up top.'

At eight hundred feet we came in through the cloud patches over the reefs and coconut palms of western Tongatapu and out over the lagoon of Nuku'alofa. With an hour added to the Fiji clock, it was already nearly nine a.m. in Tonga. Memories came flooding back as I looked down. We landed on the reef-strewn lagoon, watching through the spray-splashed windows as the coral heads passed mercifully by.

Traffic control in those days was mobile and economical. On

33

the rare occasions of an RNZAF flying-boat visit, the Superintendent of Telegraphs and Telephones was transformed into Regional
Flight Controller (Tonga). About an hour before the aircraft was
due, he would load up his wireless transmitter and receiver into
the back of a Ford pick-up van and set off to the fringes of the
grass landing strip at Fua'amotu (if a DC-3 was coming in) or the
harbour front (if it was a Sunderland or Solent flying-boat). He
would then 'talk down' the aircraft, watch till it had safely landed,
pack up and go off again until it departed. Then the reverse
procedure . . .

Nuku'alofa (the city of love, as the tourist guide books say) was
wrapped in a silence so complete that it could almost be felt.
Black, black, all black – the people, the Palace, the Royal Chapel,
buildings, offices, and houses, draped in vestments of unrelenting
mourning. Conversation only in whispers if speech could not be
avoided . . .

A genuinely heart-felt message of condolence from Buckingham
Palace had just been received by Crown Prince Tungi:

I am deeply grieved to hear of the death of Her Majesty Queen
Salote, and wish you and your people to know that I share your
sorrow in the passing of a great lady at the end of a most distinguished reign. My husband and I have happy memories of our
meetings with Queen Salote, both here and in Tonga.

Her friendship for Britain at all times and her gracious personality have endeared her to my people and your loss will be felt here
as much as in her own beloved country.

My thoughts are with you and your people in this time of
sorrow.

Elizabeth R

4

Monarch Magnificent

April 1966

A few months later, I put together three radio scripts for the New Zealand Broadcasting Corporation.

. . . Tongan history can be traced back through the royal lineage to the tenth century; and there were, until the nineteenth century, separate lines of spiritual kings, the Tu'i Tonga, and temporal kings, the Tu'i Kanokupolu and Tu'i Ha'atakalaua. The Tu'i Tonga were lords of the soil and enjoyed divine honours by virtue of their supposedly immortal origin. Later, the temporal lines emerged and it is from these that the present royal dynasty descends. By the middle of the nineteenth century, the Kingdom had been united under George Tupou I, the first Christian King and the father of modern Tonga. And so were swept aside the old beliefs and the customary institutions that depended on them. Today, every Tongan is both Christian and literate, and Tonga is the only land where the Methodist Church is the state Church.

Continuity of leadership marks the destiny of nations and people. From the nature of it stems national pride, thence a sense of identity and stability. The people of Tonga have been blessed in this respect. King George Tupou I had laid the foundation of a modern state during a reign of over forty-seven years from 1845–93. He was succeeded by George Tupou II; and he, in turn, by his daughter, Salote Mafile'o Pilolevu on 5 April 1918.

She was a slender handsome girl with a captivating smile which never left her. But her early life had been afflicted by tragedy. Her mother had died when Salote was only two years old. At eleven, she left Tonga to attend the Diocesan School for Girls in Auckland; she returned to her homeland to marry, at the age of seventeen. Six months later her father died and, heavy with child, she found herself Queen three weeks after her eighteenth birthday.

The milestones of personal bereavement continued. Her second son died in 1936 at the age of seventeen; her husband died prematurely in 1941; and her half-brother and ADC, Vilai, was

35

The Royal Tongan Lineage: An Outline

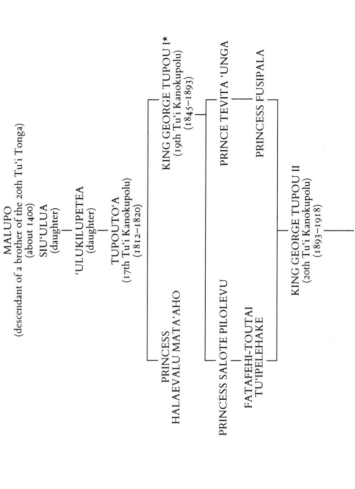

MALUPO
(descendant of a brother of the 20th Tu'i Tonga)
(about 1400)

SIU'ULUA
(daughter)

'ULUKILUPETEA
(daughter)

TUPOUTO'A
(17th Tu'i Kanokupolu)
(1812–1820)

KING GEORGE TUPOU I*
(19th Tu'i Kanokupolu)
(1845–1893)

PRINCE TEVITA 'UNGA

PRINCESS FUSIPALA

PRINCESS
HALAEVALU MATA'AHO

PRINCESS SALOTE PILOLEVU

FATAFEHI-TOUTAI
TU'IPELEHAKE

KING GEORGE TUPOU II
(20th Tu'i Kanokupolu)
(1893–1918)

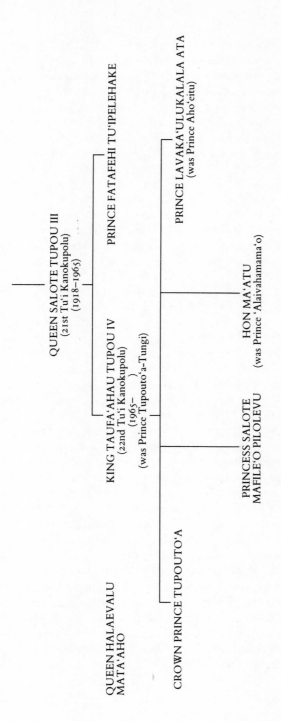

QUEEN SALOTE TUPOU III
(21st Tu'i Kanokupolu)
(1918–1965)

PRINCE FATAFEHI TU'IPELEHAKE

PRINCE LAVAKA'ULUKALALA ATA
(was Prince Aho'eitu)

KING TAUFA'AHAU TUPOU IV
(22nd Tu'i Kanokupolu)
(1965–   )
(was Prince Tupouto'a-Tungi)

HON MA'ATU
(was Prince 'Alaivahamama'o)

PRINCESS SALOTE
MAFILE'O PILOLEVU

QUEEN HALAEVALU
MATA'AHO

CROWN PRINCE TUPOUTO'A

★ The 18th Tu'i Kanokupolu was Tupouto'a's uncle, succession in the Kanokupolu line of kings until George Tupou I's constitution being by appointment immediately before the death of the reigning Tu'i Kanokupolu.

accidentally electrocuted in 1955. For years, the Queen was the victim of diabetes and for the last twelve months of her life, she lived in the almost constant agony of cancer. For all this, her composure and achievements are the more remarkable.

Her detailed knowledge of her subjects and their kinship groups was extraordinary. She knew and could elucidate the family tree and intricate relationships of her nobles and lesser chiefs. She could name fathers, mothers, cousins and offspring of numerous others. Her decision was constantly sought in respect of land ownership and boundary disputes. The Queen was concerned that her personal knowledge should not be lost and, in 1955, she set up a Traditions Committee, the object of which was to record custom and genealogy for posterity. She rightly feared that when she died, her store of knowledge would die with her, if it were not written down by those of her people who shared her recognition of its value to the survival of the Tongan way of life.

It is tempting to be over-sentimental about Queen Salote in retrospect. It was impossible not to feel captivated by her during her lifetime. There were some who came to Nuku'alofa doubting what they would find. Afterwards, their reaction was the same. Heads of state, admirals, politicians, generals, all issued from the throne room at the Palace in admiration of the Queen of Tonga. There was never a hint of condescension in her regal splendour on formal occasions. But matching it was a disarming girlish charm. They were rare complementary attributes.

Whether she spoke in English or Tongan, her voice had a compelling warmth and softness (which her granddaughter Princess Pilolevu has inherited) unassuming yet unmistakably authoritative. To hear her speak without seeing her made it hard to believe that English was her second language; and limpid dignity of style was the hallmark of her personal writings . . .

. . . Queen Salote was succeeded on 16 December 1965 by her elder son Tupouto'a Tungi, who was proclaimed as King Taufa-'ahau Tupou IV. With Australian university arts and law degrees, widely travelled, and with an insatiable interest in the up-to-date and the more efficient, the new King was eminently fitted to succeed his mother, as worldwide economic and social pressures began to be felt in Tonga. There was a new style for new needs. Prince Tungi had become Premier in 1949 at the age of thirty-one. The economic development of his country became his major preoccupation over the next decade and beyond . . .

A quarter of a century later, in Nuku'alofa, I spoke with noble 'Akau'ola, police sergeant in the 1960s and now – not unusually in Tonga – Minister of Police like his father before him.

'When Queen Salote died in 1965,' he said, 'it was not just the end of an era. It seemed the end of the Tongan world, as we knew it then. You see, Her Majesty was deeply loved by all the people of her country. Crown Prince Tungi was respected for his education and for what he was. Respected, yes, even feared by some, but not loved. Not then anyway. We were all in awe of his paramount status in Tongan history. It seemed that he was the Tu'i Tonga, Tu'i Ha'atakalaua and Tu'i Kanokupolu all in one. Which, of course, he was.'

It was not only by her own people that Queen Salote was deeply loved. The British public had taken her to their hearts on the occasion of her brief and famous visit to Britain in 1953. What happened then, on the occasion of the Coronation of Queen Elizabeth II, not only hit British press headlines, tabloids and heavies alike, but is now entrenched in Tongan folklore. When I talked with the present-day youth of Tonga about Queen Salote, something I had overlooked soon became apparent to me. To young Tongans, Queen Salote and the era she represents in their history are now almost as remote from the contemporary scene as the nineteenth-century days of King George Tupou I. And this is why I am going to relate once more the story of Queen Salote in London. After all, that is precisely what happens at night round the *kava* bowls in the villages of Tonga. There, stories lose nothing by their retelling. It is not only children who want their favourite tales told over and over again.

In March 1953, Queen Salote set out on her first and what was to be her only journey to Britain and Europe. She arrived at Southampton unknown and unheralded. None the less, she commanded interest and speculation from the moment of her arrival. She was the only reigning monarch and queen to attend the Coronation; and, as the press liked to describe her, she was the tallest queen of the smallest kingdom. Above all, her infectious charm cast a spell wherever she went.

The high point came as in the pouring rain, her open carriage drove through the cheering crowds from Westminster Abbey. There she was, the Queen of Tonga, waving a damp handkerchief and mopping her dripping forehead. Withal, her royal smile – a smile that was to light up the corridors of conversation throughout Britain that night and for a long time to come.

Queen Salote thus became the outstanding overseas figure at the Coronation. Later, in England, Northern Ireland and Europe, she left an indelible impression of majestic friendliness. Such was her popularity that songs were composed in her honour, a racehorse was named after her, and June babies were christened Charlotte.

She had, of course, a Tongan way of responding to the warmth of her welcome. *'Ofa* is the Tongan word for love; and *'ofeina* is the love shown to a stranger in another land. When her second daughter-in-law, Princess Melenaite, gave birth to a daughter, the Queen was invited to select a name for her new grandchild. Still in England at that time, Queen Salote chose 'Ofeina – meaning, in this case, the love shown to her by the people of the United Kingdom. In this way, the memory of her visit has been perpetuated in the royal house of Tonga.

The reaction of her people to Queen Salote's popular acclaim in Britain was understandably more composed than that of the Coronation crowds which greeted her. Yet there was a thirst for detailed description and eye-witness verification of the fervour of Queen Salote's reception by the British. The Tonga of 1953 had no newspaper or radio and, apart from an official daily news-sheet, no public news medium of any kind existed. Many were the tales that were passed on through village and island by word of mouth.

Weeks later, in a village near Nuku'alofa, the talk drifted round to Queen Salote's personal triumph in the Coronation procession and I was asked about her drive through the chill London rain. When I confirmed what had been told them by others, a relative of the Queen who had remained silent during the conversation looked up and spoke.

'Yes, when I heard about our Queen driving in the rain through the streets of London, I knew immediately why Her Majesty had done this. In the old days, as you know, the form of public salutation to our chiefs was to drop everything you were carrying and to crouch at the roadside with the head sunk between the knees. Even now, if a high chief passes, we should dismount from a horse or bicycle, remove a hat and lower an umbrella. It is our Queen who has taught us love and respect for the customs of our land; and Her Majesty has shown us how she too follows them though she be far from her people.'

Much was written about Queen Salote's historic ride in the

London rain. None of it provided the Queen's reason for her action. It was this.

Queen Elizabeth was travelling in a closed coach; accordingly, rain or no rain, the Queen of Tonga would decline to have her own carriage covered, in spite of the uncomprehending discomfort of the Malay Sultan travelling with her. Neither the thousands who applauded her nor the commentators who warmed to her could have known that her action in London was an expression of royal Tongan humility. To have done otherwise would have infringed the customs of which the Queen was both the repository and the pillar.

One afternoon at Her Majesty's Palace, I remembered the explanation given to me and asked the Queen whether it was correct.

'Yes,' she said, 'it is. Though I was in London, I still felt and thought as a Tongan; and in our custom, I would never cover my carriage in a procession with Her Majesty Queen Elizabeth II, no matter how wet and cold I might be. You see, in the Tongan way, no one may draw attention to himself or make a disturbance in the presence of a person of higher rank. You will understand if I tell you one or two stories to illustrate what I mean.

'When I was about six years old, I accompanied my father, the King, on a journey to Ha'apai and Vava'u. We arrived at Ha'ano in Ha'apai, and on the afternoon when we came to leave it was found that the anchor had been caught under a rock. The men from Ha'ano started diving for the anchor, and an old man called 'Aisea was one of them. 'Aisea was so concerned about this mishap to the King's journey that he continued to search for the elusive anchor and, apparently overcome with exhaustion, he did not reappear. No one knew what had befallen him until his lifeless body floated to the surface.

'I remember, too, a day about a year later when I was returning from the ceremony of the dedication of a new boat. Travelling in the carriage behind me was the grandmother of Tuna 'Ulukalala Ata, the wife of the present Minister of Police. As they turned a corner, the third finger of her right hand was caught in the cartwheel and severed save for a shred of skin. She uttered no cry of pain and I first learned about it when I was told that she had gone for medical attention.

'In 1918 I visited Ha'alaufuli in Vava'u shortly after I had become Queen. We were walking to the village when a swarm of hornets, which I suppose we had disturbed, descended upon one of my attendants. When we arrived I noticed her face was puffed up and I asked her what had happened. She told me she had been attacked by hornets.

41

'"Didn't they hurt you?" I asked.

'"Yes," she replied, "but I could not cry out while I was following Your Majesty."

'Then,' continued Queen Salote, 'there is a story which has now become almost legendary in our history. In 1852, the town of Pea in Tongatapu was under siege by the warriors of Ha'apai led by King George Tupou I. Inside were people who opposed the adoption of Christianity. Suddenly a spear, hurled from the fort, went through the abdomen of one of the King's men whose name was Liemalohi. The King turned to him and said, "Lie, you are wounded." Although in great distress, Lie broke the spear leaving the spearhead inside and replied, "Your Majesty, it is not words but deeds that count!"

'When the battle had been won, King George asked Lie what he would wish done for him. Lie replied, "As long as I can see again the white sand of the beach at Ha'apai, I will know that I have reached home, and will die in peace in the knowledge that I have done my duty."

'So sail was set for Ha'apai; and when Lie was shown the white sand he pulled the spearhead out of his body and surrendered himself to death. He was buried at his village of Koulo where the name Liemalohi is still an appointed title, whose origin is in this story of great bravery in battle.'

The Queen smiled gravely and paused. Then that sense of girlish fun, always bubbling below her regal dignity, burst through.

'There's another little story that I haven't been indiscreet enough to tell anyone yet.' Her eyes sparkled as she laughed.

'I was so sorry for the Sultan. He was cold and miserable in the rain and at last he could stand it no longer.

'"Rain. Cold. Get wet. Close roof," he pleaded, as he crouched in his corner of our damp carriage and tried to persuade me to agree to what he wanted.

'I was naughty. "No understand. No speak English," I replied and looked as if I did not appreciate what he was talking about.

'At last, the poor Sultan gave in and stayed silent and unhappy for the rest of our journey. I hope that he does not think too ill of me now.'

So the Queen of Tonga, whose mastery of elegant English was complete, drove on uncovered through the Coronation rain.

There is a postscript. Later that year Queen Elizabeth and the Duke of Edinburgh landed at the solitary jetty at Nuku'alofa in the course of their first round-the-world journey and their first visit to Tonga.

As they came ashore and entered an open car, rain began to fall. Queen Salote opened an umbrella and held it over Queen Elizabeth only. The two Queens looked at each other and laughed. The spirit of the Coronation procession had come from London for another royal ride in the rain, on this occasion in the heart of Polynesia.

5

A Sort of Third Coming

February 1991

This time all would be different. Thirty-eight years lay between my first sea landing and my present aerial descent. Not that there is any special significance in that, given the supposed timelessness of Tongan society, culture and traditions. But the period does, of course, embrace those years in which there have been the most sustained external influences on that society and the greatest changes within it.

An hour away from landing, I picked up another airline brochure. Title: *The Kingdom of Tonga*. Great photographs. Good layout. But the accompanying text . . .

'. . . Every morning in these amiable, leisurely islands dawns a fresh beginning, yet with a feeling of timelessness, a soothing, predictable rhythm drawing its strength from the eternal verities . . .' (I'd had one of those strength-giving eternal verities for breakfast that morning. It is usually called cornflakes.) '. . . For Tonga makes no attempt to emulate the high-tension high-decibel living of more sophisticated countries, a fact reflected in its people's gentle, smiling friendliness . . .'

Not, I thought, much enlightenment as to why, in twenty-five years, some 60,000 Tongans – more than half the present population – have sought to escape their desert island disco land for a new life in New Zealand, Australia, Hawaii, California and, earlier, Fiji. But perhaps this sort of platitudinous gush goes some way towards explaining how it is that, in reverse, Tonga continues to attract toe-in-the-water senior citizens, surging ashore from the occasional cruise liner and aeroplane, and clutching their first-time passports for travel out of New Zealand and Australia. Plus, increasingly, Hawaii-sated Americans yearning for an evening with Bloody Mary in a touristically virginal South Pacific; and to take the story of it all back to the potatoes of Idaho.

Thus, through judiciously condoned emigration and modest tourism expectations, both Tongan economy and society retain a semblance of stability, with a worldwide survival kit, cushioned and

44

supported by those thousands of Tongans whose expatriation from their homeland enhances their devotion to it; and their continuing acceptance, from afar, of the perceived thraldom from which they sought, as a motive for their departure, to escape. Distance in this case does, it seems, lend enchantment; and absence surely makes the Polynesian heart grow fonder. Out of sight of his island country is not, for the expatriate Tongan, out of mind: like the accepted need to send remittances to the family back home. I was given a figure of T$40 million per annum as Tonga's income from these remittances. You see the beneficiaries assembling outside the Bank of Tonga on Monday mornings, clutching their precious envelopes with New Zealand, Australian and American dollar bank notes inside.

The past is always with them and us, nudging the present. Getting in the way, some would say, with antiquated customs, onerous traditions and outmoded social demands. So newer generations, at least, might view them.

When I was at Auckland University College, as it then was, I read history. I was thus known as an historian, for reasons that escaped me then and still do, especially since I have long since come to distrust those historians whose predilection it is for making largely unprovable judgments about past actions and motives, using the quite different standards of the present to do so.

Peter France puts it well in the introduction to his *The Charter of the Land – Custom and Colonisation in Fiji*:

The tendency of historical research in each generation is to reveal the prejudices and misconceptions of an earlier age without always being fully conscious of its own . . . The hindsight that enables us to delineate the bias of our predecessors is as much a product of a realignment of prejudices as of an increase in understanding.

His own eclectic approach was characterised as 'one of empirical scepticism after the manner of the Fijian chief who, when asked to explain the customs of his tribe in the matter of chiefly succession, replied that the custom was to fight about it.'

And that, in essence, is what happened to Fiji, decades later, in 1987 when two military coups overthrew a democratically elected government of mainly western Fijians and Indians and re-entrenched eastern chiefly authority. As Anthony Lester said in the course of a

1989 BBC TV debate on 'The State of Democracy': 'All power is delightful, but absolute power is absolutely delightful.'

To those who hold it, that is. Which is broadly what the argument is all about in contemporary Tonga.

6

It All Depends on Where You Sit

I thought again about the vacuous flapdoodle of that airline brochure – a little more kindly this time. After all, in the past, Tongans have written and, when encouraged, have spoken about themselves in similar vein. They did not question the durability of their self-assumed impregnable role as the bastion of custom and indigenous tradition in the South Pacific; or its unchanging character.

In so doing the Tongan has been justified, at least in part. The islands not only lack a colonial past: the people are quietly smug about the fact that they successfully engineered their avoidance of it. The jibe that Tongans are the ethnic and cultural snobs of the South Pacific may be well founded; for they care not a jot for the occasional discomfort in such matters of some of their regional neighbours.

I wrote a first, innocent book on Tonga and the Tongans in 1954. The Polynesian world, like everywhere else for that matter, was more than a little different then.

Tevita Tu'ipulotu Toutaiolepo was then the Supreme Court interpreter and translator. This is what he wrote in the introduction to that book, with a title heading provided by Queen Salote herself:

Ko E Mo'ui 'A E Kakai Tonga – The Tongan Way Of Life

We Tongans are a branch of the Polynesian race which inhabits the islands of the Central and Eastern Pacific. Our origins are lost in the mists of antiquity but we have been living in these islands for a very long time as evidenced by the knowledge we have of our ancient kings which has been handed down through the centuries by word of mouth from generation to generation.

Endowed by nature with a strong physique, amply proportioned but not ungainly, with a broad nose, dark straight hair, dark eyes, and a skin the colour of rich cinnamon, the Tongan has a characteristic slowness of movement which, it has been said, gives him a natural dignity. The Tongan woman has rounded features and dark expressive eyes, and to keep the smooth soft texture of her skin she rubs her body with coconut oil.

Our isolation and environment have evolved for us a way of

47

life and an outlook peculiarly suited to our simple needs which
contact with Western civilisation has changed but little. The men
occupy their time in building houses, carving canoes, growing
foodstuffs and in looking after domestic pigs and fowls; while the
women care for the children, attend to household tasks, prepare
bark cloth, plait mats and weave baskets. Our closeness to the
heart of nature has made us resourceful, self-reliant, independent
and intensely loyal to our land.

A distinctive feature of the Tongan character is respect for the
chiefs: this respect is deep rooted and springs from ancient religious
belief. Its influence on our life is profound, dictating our standard
of conduct, and making social demands on our everyday inter-
course. To merit this respect the chiefs observe a standard of propriety and conduct befitting their chiefly position; and this respect
is the foundation of our great love for our Queen.

In these beautiful islands our gift for song and poetry finds ready
expression. We ease the burden of our daily tasks by singing; there
is a song for the launching and the beaching of a canoe, for the
dragging of a heavy log from the forest to the house site. Great
events and notable personages in our history are commemorated
in song and poetry. There is a song for welcome and another for
farewell. When a village maiden is wooed, her suitors ply their
plaints in song and verse.

The Christian religion, too, now plays an important part in our
life. The sacredness of the Sabbath is strictly observed as a day of
worship when we may not work or play; and because we love our
Church a great part of our time is absorbed in its activities. From
work in the gardens or fishing on the reef we return to the village
as evening approaches for a meeting or choir practice. To the
village pastor, the people turn for spiritual comfort and consolation
in times of distress and sorrow.

In a life in which money and time are of little moment we have
learnt to love the simple things which are part of that life – the
warm drenching sunlight, the beauty of the dawn and sunset, the
sound of song and laughter in the still night, the innumerable
murmurings of the reef, the moonlight on the lagoon – and in
loving them we find peace and contentment.

I was gratified and delighted by this at the time. It seemed to sum
up in clear sonorous English all that the Tonga of Queen Salote
represented and all that was distinctively and serenely Tongan. Or
at least how Tongans then liked to depict it and what appeared to

FARE PURCHASE:
Tonga's
King Taufa'ahau
Tupou and
a favoured cab

Taxi, to Tonga please!

by DAVID WILLIAMS

THE King of Tonga is keeping up his reputation as a trendy follower of fashion — by ordering his own London black cab.

The monarch, tracking the footsteps of Prince Philip, Lord King, Sir Andrew Lloyd Webber and the Governor General of Turks and Caicos, has chosen his own version — his second — of the famous workhorse.

The order, with LTI Carbodies of Coventry, was signed by the Crown Prince, but it is believed the King himself will use the vehicle as his official transport.

LTI craftsmen are fitting leather upholstery, air-conditioning — and a seat for a bodyguard — in the £30,000 vehicle, to be shipped to the Pacific island in July.

"The Prince was impressed when he saw the cabs in London," said an LTI spokesman. "The Ton-gan Royal family already had fond memories of London cabs — they ordered a similar model 20 years ago."

The king is reportedly still impressed by the partition separating passengers from the driver. But he wasn't so keen on the "For Hire" sign, which will be left off.

The order is just the tip of an export boom for LTI Carbodies, which was formed in 1919 and now employs 300.

The firm, more used to a trickle of overseas orders from countries like Kenya and Japan, will soon announce a 60-cab, £1.2 million order for Taipei, Taiwan.

Other countries to have jumped on the taxi bandwagon include France, Romania and Brazil.

e-mail: citydesk@e

147
130
200
733# −1
163#
3¾
289 +4
77#
320
123

FIED IALS
146
0⁹/₁₆ +¹/₃₂
11½# −1½
122
59¼ −1¼
958# +1
307#
195½ −2
146#
542½
190½ −1
430 −2
133#
17½
173# +2
229 −1
169# −1
263 +1
50½
300# +4
514¼ −5¼
327# +2

CITY
625 −10
808 −18
424 −9
197 −1½
535 −4
400 −5
632 −22
433 −7
544 −5
404 −4
346 +1
367 +1
829 −15
812 −17

CAL ENT
265 +8
289
194 +1
42½# −1½
338# +3
14# +1
35
27¾ −¼
47½
817
790 −15
142# −1
49#
36#
80 +2
612 −2
663 +1
51½
132#
33 −1
238
27# +3
135#
130 +1
37/16 −3/8
184#
11 11/32 +5/32
336 +1
286 −1
676 −12
240
435
154
232

RING
94#
112
185#
818 +50
130
114
5 15/16 +1/8
554
43
129
859 −4

Renishaw 480
Renold 298½
Richsn West .... 78#
Rolls R .... 221# −3
Rotork .... 238#
Senior Eng .... 107#
Siebe .... 833 −10

600 Grp 270
Smiths Ind .... 688# −9
Spirax S .... 733#
TI .... 551# +1
Tex Hldgs 50
Transfer Tech 120
Triplex Lloyd 173
Vickers .... 252 −3
Vitec 748
Vspr Thrnycrft .. 823
Wagon Ind .... 418 −4
Weir .... 255# −1
Wellman 53½
Whatman .... 398# +3

ENGINEERING VEHICLES
AAF Industrial ....29 −1
Avon .... 626 +28
B B A .... 332# −4
B S G .... 75¾ +¼
Benson Gp .... 43* −1
ERF 234
GKN .... 965# −11
Laird .... 487# −1
Lucas .... 227# −6½
T & N .... 171# +2

FOOD MANFS
Acatos & Hutch .250
Albert Fisher .. 52# +1
A B Foods .... 376 −6
Avonmore .... 148#
Banks Sidney 288
Barr A G .... 332 +2
Benson Crisps .. 29
Booker .... 391# −2
Borthwick .... 30½ −½
Cadbury Schw 492½#
.... −13½
Canadian Pizza . 81# −1
Carrs Milling 325
Cavaghan 95
Cranswick 197
Dalgety .... 378# −2
Daniels S 32
Devro Intl .... 233#

HOUSEHOLD GOODS
Airsprung 224
Cornwell Pk A ... 120
Gaskell 148
Jeyes Grp .... 142 +1
Lionhart 0½

Oriflame 520
Paterson Zoch .. 455
Reckitt & C .... 707# −4
Relyon 327
Silentnight 208
Stoddard 25
Tams (John) 57
Tomkinson 235
Walker G 99

INSURANCE
Archer .... 63 +3
Bradstock 72
Comm Union ... 603# −2
Fenchurch .... 123 +2
G R E .... 266# −2
Gen Acc .... 630 −4
Heath C E 97
Hiscox Select... 124
Independnt Ins.497# −10
JIB Group .... 116#
Lwnds Lmbrt 144
Masthead .... 112 +1
Nelson Hurst...197#
Ockham .... 55 −1
Oriel .... 143 +6
Royal .... 422 −2
Sedgwick .... 147 −1
Steel BUR Jons . 46#
Sun Alliance ... 401# −1
Willis Corroon .. 150 −2
Windsor 20

INVESTMENT TRUSTS
3i .... 456 −3
Alliance .... £21 23/32 −3/32
Ang Oseas .... 496 −4
Bankers Inv .... 227# −2½
Brit Assets .... 97 −1
Brit Inv .... 231 +2
Dunedin Sm 368½
Edinburgh Inv ... 332 −2
Electra .... 401 −2
Fleming Merc..331½ −3
Flemng Overses 346 −3½
Foreign & C .... 159¾ −2¾
GT Inc Growth ... 97 −1

Unichem .... 254# +3

HOUSEHOLD GOODS
Rank Org .... 539 +7
Regal .... 53 −1
Ryan .... 46# +1
Savoy £13 13/32
Stakis .... 108 +1½
Stanley Leisure..474 −1
Tandem 15

Thorn EMI ... £17 19/32 −9/32
Tomorrow Leisre 7½ +1½
Tottenham 370*
Vardon .... 129 −1
Wembley 370
Zetters 122

LIFE ASSURANCE
Britannic .... 785# −4
Legal & Gen .... 726# −1½
Liberty Intl 378
Lloyds Abbey ... 525 −1
Ldn & Man .... 405# −3
Pru .... 439# −5
Refuge .... 535# −3
Utd Friendly ... 808# −6

MEDIA
Abbott Mead .... 582 +2
Avesco 218
Blenheim Grp ... 331 +2
Border TV 278
Bristol E Post 385
B Sky B .... 452 −2
Capital Radio .... 664 −2
Carlton C .... 467 +8
Chrysalis 485
Cordiant 135
CIA Gp .... 180#
Crown Comm .. 6 SP
Daily Mail A..£16 11/32
EMAP 678
HTV .... 369#
Hodder Head.. 260#
Media Bus 5½
Mirror Group ... 236# −1
More O'Ferrall . 624#
News Intl .... 324 −2
Pearson .... 702# +14
Phonelink 189
Portsmouth Snd.623
Reed Int .... £11 9/16 −3/32
Reuters .... 747 +2
Scot Radio 333
Scot TV .... 696# −1
Shandwick 56½
Sleepy Kid .... 30# −3

Rackwood 53
Vaal Reef £67 13/32
.... +1
WattsBike .... 535#
Zandpan 44

OILS
Arcon Intl 33
Aviva 34
BP .... 562½ −
Brit Borneo .... 543# −
Brmah Castrol £10⅜ −
Cairn 224
Central Pacific ... 165
Clyde .... 64#
Edinburgh Oil 23
Enterprise .... 431#
Evergreen 404
−
Gt West Res 18
Hardy Oil 245
Lasmo 187
Monument Oil ... 68¼
PittencrieffRs 55
Premier .... 31½#
Presidio .... 11 SP
Ramco Energy ...595
Ranger 490
Royal Dtch ..£92 13/32

Seafield Res 88
Shell Trans ... 851½# −
Tullow 88½
Unit Energy 15
Vanguard Pet ... 13¾
Woodside 395

OTHER FINANCIAL
Berry BCH 35
Caledonia 799
Cater Allen 413
Cattles .... 270#
Clayhithe 70
Gerrard Nat 394
Henderson ... £11 9/32
Invesco .... 242# −
Ivory and S 244
King & Sh 163
Lon Forfait 285
M & G .... £12½# −
M A I 450
Prov Fin 977
SJP Cap 119
Swire Pac 533
Union 93

OTHER SERVICES
Anglo Unt 0½
Anglo Eastern .. 122#
Applied Holog ... 123
Bertam 295
Black Arrow 46
Caird 226
Cosalt 180
Filofax 252
Greenway 66
Hozelock 551
Leigh Int 105
Nobo Grp 130
Photo-Me 159
Scapa Group 237
Shanks McEwan 105
Sinclair Wm 211
UDO Holdings . 242#

PHARMACEUTICAL
Glxo Wllcom . 771½# −
Grampian .... 134#
Huntingdon Int 95
Medeva .... 249#
Smithkl Bchm . 648½
Zeneca .... £13 23/32 +

PRINT & PAPER
API Gp 635
Arjo Wiggins .... 183#
Aspen Comm 270
Bemrose 392
Blagden In .... 170#
Brit Poly .... 760#
Bunzl .... 236#
Cradley 52
Crest Packaging .. 69
De La Rue 729
Delyn 84
Dolphin .... 165#
Fairway Grp 93
Jarvis Porter 292
Low-Bonar 552
MY Holdings ....97#
REXAM .... 379#
St Ives .... 485#
Sidlaw 108

accord with or confirm my own contemporary perceptions: languor-
ous sunsets and assured spiritual salvation – for Tongans.

So had the myth become the reality or was the reality just a myth?
In 1954 I was happy to leave things as they were written without
questioning the apparently authentic voice of self-analysis and self-
portrayal, even though I knew, deep down, that the facts were beginning to suggest otherwise.

Such superficial detachment is no longer possible, except in the
tourist brochures. In the past decade or so, other Tongans – aca-
demics, lawyers, editors, poets and parliamentarians – have written
and spoken very differently about a system which mercifully permits
them to do so but which few appear now to appraise either through
the rose-tinted spectacles of the past or in isolation from the influences at work elsewhere in the world. Indeed, it is a welcome accomplishment that Tongans today are articulate, critical, questioning (in
at least two languages) and far from customarily docile. Yet their
singular institutions – the constitution, the monarchy, the Church,
the language, the sense of corporate *fiefia* – remain, if not unchanged,
outwardly intact. And so much the better. To demythologise (that
ugly word) is not, I think, for me, at least at this stage in these
proceedings.

> I count among the Tongans so many true friends that it would
> touch me nearly if I should seem in the following pages to have
> been lacking in recognition of their admirable qualities. If I have
> spoken of their institutions with levity, it is because I have judged
> the nation from the standard of a European people, with whom,
> in intelligence, physique, and disposition, they are fit to be com-
> pared. I have printed these pages with the knowledge and per-
> mission of the chiefs best fitted to speak for the whole people; and
> when I refuse to treat seriously the fatal experiment of engrafting
> Western customs upon their own ancient and admirable polity, I
> am only reproducing the sense of grotesqueness with which their
> present hybrid institutions inspire the best of them. Where I have
> laughed, they have laughed with me; what I have deplored, they
> have no less regretted.

Thus Basil Thomson, in his *Diversions of a Prime Minister*, November
1894.

Well then, was it a 'fatal experiment'? Perhaps we shall discover
how it all seems a century or so later.

7

Literary Lapse

November 1990

'You could, of course, do a travel book on Tonga. The old biddies haven't forgotten Queen Salote and that Coronation ride in the London rain. Now that Sydney is next door for Walsall grandmothers on Apex, European tourism is getting curious about the South Seas again. New horizons and all that. Tiki Tours and Marco Polo are doing great. Same part of the world, more or less.'

He was a London literary agent, comfortably expansive with, he said, a Maori on his staff. A salesman whose death had not yet been announced, he sat luxuriating in a Liberace glitter-jacket. Enough to date him – and me, I thought, and his semi-deaf receptionist.

'That is, if it's your style of thing. There isn't one on Tonga that I know of. But I'll ask my Maori.'

He shuffled his feet and the papers on his desk top. 'Never know from one minute to another whom I get in that chair.'

I looked around. There was only one. I was in it.

'Oh?'

'Yes. Last week it was . . .' He gave the name of a luminary of the British judiciary. 'I've agreed to take on his autobiography. Unseen. Exciting, that. Rather rare.' He looked towards his bookshelves. 'I still handle the literary estate of that chap.' He waved vaguely at some expensively bound titles. 'My father got him originally. In the United States, of course. A London taxi driver came in the week before. His story wasn't at all bad. For a London taxi driver. I took that too. So what have you got?'

I opened my briefcase and produced a couple of hardbacks. 'No, no, no, not what you've done. What you're going to do.'

His telephone erupted. 'I'll be right down. You will excuse me, won't you? Important reception. There are so many publishers I have to attend upon at this time of year. Before we all go off to the Frankfurt book circus. Think about what I've said. Find a round-the-world airline that puts down in Tonga and get them interested. How kind of you to look in. Leave your pieces of paper. I'm sure you'll do something.'

Are you, I thought, as I stepped carefully past the cardboard boxes and genuflected before the semi-deaf receptionist who was now apparently blind and dumb too. Not much of Liberace about all this – except the jacket. And the fact that there isn't a round-the-world airline route that includes Tonga as a stop-over point. You have to go via Auckland or Fiji and take a side trip. Or did then in 1990. Now Air New Zealand has Tonga on its round-the-world ticketing.

I had made the reservations to Auckland and from Auckland to Tonga in a wintry Sevenoaks. The county of Kent had for once missed the worst of the January gales and snowstorms which swept through Wales, the Midlands and much of Scotland. But it was still bleak, wet, cold and windy. The South Pacific seemed more compelling by the hour. The continuing misfortunes of England's cricketers in Australia should have been a bit less unbearable in a down-under summer sun. But, as usual, they weren't.

It seemed appropriate to undertake the last leg of my journey with Polynesian Airlines (not that it is Tongan; it is the airline of Western Samoa), and in spite of the fact that the word for aeroplane in both the Tongan and Fijian tongues means flying-boat or canoe. Well it might, I had thought, as the creaking Sunderland lurched into the air from the lagoon on my last journey; but was not, I hoped, going to be right for a Boeing 72S. Unless that 'S' had a more sinister implication such as 'seaplane'. I looked out of the window. No water-skis were visible. I reached under the seat. The life jacket was safely in place; the captain and navigator comfortingly Polynesian. If the compass went wildly wrong (as once happened to a Pan-American trans-Pacific clipper flight which came down at Pago Pago instead of Honolulu) they ought to be able to fall back on ancient skills and plot their course by the stars. I did not think it necessary to tell them that there was a reserve navigator – of sorts – on board their flying canoe.

In the seventeenth century there lived a chief called Tuita who was renowned throughout the land for his skill in seamanship and navigation. Tuita often ventured as far afield as Fiji, Samoa and the Wallis Islands. On these occasions he used the *kalia* or large double canoe, across whose bridge was a hut about the size of an average living-room today. He had a crew of thirty and frequently carried about a hundred passengers.

Towards the end of a long and vigorous life (he is believed to have lived till he was well over ninety) Tuita accompanied his King on a journey to Fiji. The royal navigators, 'Akau'ola and Ula, were also the captains of the King's canoe, while Tuita, who was by this time completely blind, sailed with his son in a second canoe. On the way back from Viti Levu, the royal flotilla ran into the heavy south-east storms of the season and for ten days no land was sighted. When the weather again grew calm, the King invited his navigators to tell him where they were. Reluctantly and with shame, they confessed that they did not know; for the severity of the winds had been such that even they, the wisest and most skilled of the King's navigators, could not tell whither they should row.

Much angered by their incompetence, the King called for Tuita's canoe to draw near so that the old navigator's opinion could be sought as to how far they had progressed towards Tonga. Tuita told one of his attendants to carry him to the side of the canoe so that he could reach out and touch the water passing by. When he had done so, Tuita said to those who watched, 'We are not yet near Tonga for these are the ocean waters of Fiji.'

And when they asked, 'But how can you know?' he replied, 'I can tell by the feel of the sea.'

So Tuita pointed the way ahead and the canoes sailed on as he directed. When the day was spent, he asked his son to describe the appearance of the tropic stars and after he had heard enough, he again gave instructions for their course.

Next morning Tuita asked his son to splash the sea in his face. As he felt the texture of the water, he said, 'This is a Lakemba wave. Soon you will see the Fiji island of Lakemba which is nearly halfway on our journey to Tonga.' And so it was that in the afternoon, the palm trees of Lakemba rose out of the sea ahead, just as the blind navigator had promised.

When the King saw the island, he called Tuita's canoe and said to 'Akau'ola and Ula: 'You are the heads of my navigators, but you are the sleeping heads with eyes which do not see. From this time henceforth, the blind Tuita shall be my chief navigator.'

So they made their way safely on to Tonga, and to this day, Tuita is the head of the royal navigators.

The original Tuita had, however, another claim to fame which has given him a special place in the folklore of Tonga. In the long days of his physical virility, Tuita was renowned as a great seafaring lover.

After every virginal conquest, it was his practice to tie a knot in the long *kafa* or sinnet cord he wore round his *ta'ovala*. Married women and unmarried girls no longer in their original state of virtuous innocence were not excluded from romantic investigation, but did not qualify for record in the *kafa*. The crew of Tuita's canoe knew well what the knots in his *kafa* meant, so that when he died not many months after his honourable recognition by the King, they made haste to examine the testimony of his prowess in the art of lovemaking. They found that the *kafa* was nearly 200 yards long and that it contained exactly 3,000 knots, of which none had been tied twice.

When the chiefly successor to the title of Tuita was appointed, he was also named Tolu'afe which means 'three thousand'.

In 1954, when I knew none of this, I was in Ha'apai a short time after the English and Tongan versions of my 'Royal Visit to Tonga' had appeared. Late one night, after some local festivities, I returned to the Governor's residence to find him seated cross-legged on the verandah with a dozen or so of his retainers and an amply filled *kava* bowl. We talked until two o'clock about the glorious past of Tonga, its politics and religion, its royal wars and its royal romances.

Then Governor Fielakepa called for silence and announced his intention of bestowing upon me the name 'Tolu'afe', a title of the great navigator of the old Tu'i Tonga. And Tuita, one of Her Majesty's Nobles who was seated beside Fielakepa, nodded his assent. So it was done and I was expected to respond to their gracious but unexpected act.

'I am,' I said, 'deeply grateful; but I trust that I shall not be called upon, navigationally or otherwise, to justify my suitability for this honorary appointment.'

And not now either, I reflected, as the Boeing 72S flew on to Tonga, thirty-seven years later, in 1991.

8

The Spirit of Tonga

1 February 1991

Those close-of-day displays of fire fade fast at tropical sundown. The brilliant spectacle of a moment and they are gone. Look away and you miss the plunge to oblivion. This one dipped from an angry sky below the menace of towering cumulus, flashed its last long signals through the clouds, and expired. It seemed a sort of baptismal death.

Rain, heavy driving squalls of it, swept past the aircraft windows as we came in over the darkened reef, and down on to a tarmac surface flanked by standard airport night illumination. The control tower, just visible in the gloom, could have been in the British Virgin Islands or Cyprus.

The unwelcoming rain stepped up its fierce tempo. Arrival passengers stayed in the aircraft; fifty yards to terminal-building shelter seemed a long way. But home in Apia that night beckoned to a tired crew. It was disembarkation with gentle encouragement but no umbrellas. So we moved out slowly from beneath the wings and ran for cover.

Maybe the weather disturbed things a bit, but there was, instantly, a relaxed air of confusion. The terminal building was old, wooden, uncomfortable and disorganised. So, more or less, was I, having completed only one of the two forms (for Immigration and Customs) in the aircraft. I was duly admonished by a formidable lady with one large stripe on her uniformed arm, who appeared to personify Tongan Immigration 1991. She searched beneath her desk for a landing card. There was none. A young minion was despatched into the rain and came back from the aeroplane clutching a damp box of forms. I did my duty, filled it in on my knee and handed it over.

'How long will you be in Tonga?'

'About . . .'

'Not about. Exactly.'

'Oh. Well, exactly . . . Let me think . . . Fifty days, to be precise. If that's all right with everybody.'

The dragon raised a hefty forearm and planted a stamp heavily on my passport. A written entry and it was mine again.

GOVERNMENT OF TONGA
IMMIGRATION ACT 1969 SECT. 10
(VISITOR PERMIT)
Permitted to enter with
Temporary Entry Status
on 01-02-91
To remain for one and a half months
Employment prohibited
Fua'amotu Airport
Imm. Off. A

In terms of duration it was going to be a tight squeeze. But I liked the idea of employment prohibited and, by implication, idleness encouraged. It seemed to be saying, with a sense of history, beach-combers welcome once again. And perhaps it was understood that it was *paid* employment that was *verboten*.

'Thank you,' I said to Imm. Off. A as I moved a yard or so to a pile of wet baggage strewn all over the concrete floor. My four checked pieces were mercifully all present and correct and not about to spend a sweaty sojourn in Samoa. I had been handed a 'Health Card for all persons arriving Tonga. KEEP TONGA FREE FROM AIDS.'

OK, I said to myself. Absolutely. I'll do my bit . . . Then I looked at the bottom of the last page: 'REMEMBER. Having more than one sexual partner is very risky.'

How Tongan times have changed since those of the navigating Don Juan, Tolu'afe.

A sign on the wooden wall caught my eye. Nothing had prepared me for this piece of commercial enterprise in a new jet-propelled Tonga. It was Singapore and Sydney entrepreneurialism in the Friendly Islands.

LANDING PASSENGERS
Buy your duty-free spirits and cigarettes at the
Duty-free Shop before you go into town

I looked around, stumbled backwards over the baggage and seemed to depart from Tonga once more as I went round a corner through the rain and into a pulsating wooden enclave lined with bottles of whisky, gin, rum, vodka and cigarettes. On the other side of a half-open door, welcoming families awaited their returning relatives – and what they brought. If you could not call it a traffic exactly in duty-free loot, there was certainly a trickle being passed surreptitiously from hand to hand through the opening into the enveloping concealment of bosomy blouse and *ta'ovala* beyond.

I went back to my baggage, clutching the indicated duty-free quantities.

'Pay duty on the extra you bring in,' the notice had said. 'It will still be cheaper than at the stores in town.' How greedy we are in small things, I thought.

I put my bags on the Customs counter. Rain and sweat streamed down. Outside. Inside. It was, after all, the South Pacific hurricane season.

'Is this all your baggage?'

'Yes.'

'Have you been to Tonga before?'

'Yes.'

'You will know what to expect then.'

'Well . . . I'm not sure . . .'

'Is someone meeting you with a car?'

'Yes. I believe so.'

'You will need some help with these.' He pointed to the locked cases.

'Yes. Are there porters perhaps?'

'Not now. We'll carry them for you.'

He smiled at my surprise. Well he might, in a harsh international airport world.

But so it was that two genial uniformed Tongan Customs officers picked up my anonymous pieces of baggage and carried them, unexamined, through the exit door to the rain-swept car rank outside.

'Welcome again to Tonga. Enjoy your stay. Come again when we have the jumbos and the new terminal is opened in July on the King's seventy-third birthday. Goodbye now.'

Mud sprayed my trousers as a car drew away into the night. It did not matter. I had met my first new or old Friendly Islanders. Tonga was still Tonga. Perhaps even a bit more so.

9

Reorientation

Tongatapu is shaped like an old fairytale boot with the toe turned up – or so it seems to me. The largest of the islands of Tonga, it is of coral limestone with a low, largely flat landscape. A bit dull therefore, you could say. The highest point is the Fua'amotu Ridge which achieves the great elevation of two hundred feet. The so-called Mount Zion behind the Palace in Nuku'alofa is the highest point in the capital. It is all of fifty feet.

I spent my first night with Pierre Encontre, a talented black-browed French bureaucrat on loan via the UN as an economic adviser to the Government of Tonga. He was the proud owner of the only left-hand-drive French car on the island, a twenty-one-year-old Peugeot saloon which used to belong to his father. It had conveyed him and his new British Virgin Islands lawyer wife through southern France and into Spain on their honeymoon three years before. Now it must be doing its last tour of duty for him.

It served the purpose for the half-hour journey and for my reunion in darkness and rain with the capital, Nuku'alofa. Even in those circumstances, the essential character of the place seemed unchanged. It is not a metropolis: like the Kingdom as a whole, everything is in miniature. Beyond the public green and along the foreshore with its impressive Norfolk Island pines are the Palace grounds and the white painted wooden Palace itself. It is only a few steps from the water-front to the Post Office, the Treasury and the Philatelic Bureau; the Bank of Tonga, the shops and the market; the Legislative Assembly and the court offices. In five minutes you can reach the royal burial grounds and tombs. Nuku'alofa is completely flat. There are few gutters but its main streets are slightly raised in the centre, like the hump of a bridge, allowing the tropical rain to sluice past the low props of the wooden buildings and gather in someone's swamp-ridden back yard.

Now there are some fine new buildings, not least that of the Privy Council and Ministry of Foreign Affairs, the spacious Roman Catholic basilica and the traditionally designed Visitors' Bureau. Dotted around the town are a number of good restaurants – Italian, French, German, Indian and Chinese. Some of them operate from wooden houses, and have the same kind of intimacy and friendly charm as their characterful counterparts in New Caledonia. This modest culinary internationalism is relatively new but welcome.

The seventy-odd miles of road through the coconut and banana plantations of the island are good, but there are uncatalogued driving hazards. People born into the free movement of village life regard traffic procedures as largely unrelated to pedestrians. A yellow line is painted down the centre of the pathless main street. It was used sometimes by cyclists to see whether they could ride straight along it without falling off. This worked so long as no one else was doing the same thing in the opposite direction. It is strange that there are still Tongans who seem to ride a bicycle or drive a car with ears and eyes closed to the surrounding world.

In the country there is no generally adopted speed limit, but there are natural hazards which create their own constraints. Tonga has an abundance of pigs, none of which is amenable to prolonged captivity, and you cannot drive for more than a mile or two into the outlying villages without an old sow and some of her offspring dashing from out of the coconut trees into the centre of the road, just when you've put your foot down and are off at the fine old speed of thirty miles an hour. Adequate if fitful speed control is thus ensured; and while this may have terminal consequences for the occasional piglet or chicken, it is achieved at no expense or apparent effort on the part of authority.

Next day I went by boat the short distance to Pangaimotu, 'island of refuge', where in 1852 George Tupou I assembled his forces for the final victorious assault in the name of Christian Tonga on the resisting heathens of Tongatapu. Pangaimotu is the largest of the sand cays off Tongatapu and the closest to Nuku'alofa.

If you are brave enough, you can walk across the reef to it at low tide as the Tongans do. It is 2,000 feet long and 1,500 feet wide, encapsulating the idyllic tropic islet – lush vegetation, flowers and fruit in abundance, coconuts and pawpaws by the score, a shallow sandy beach surround and pellucid, welcoming, silky water. It belongs to the King and a small relaxing day resort is managed with dextrous versatility and infinite patience by my youngest brother-in-law, Earle Pangia Emberson. The Gulf War seemed light years away.

I stayed there for my first six nights, gazing in fresh wonderment at the cooling splendours of the daily sunsets beyond the lights of Nuku'alofa's cinemascopic waterfront. Then I moved to Papiloa's

Place (the Friendly Islander motel on Tongatapu) to write on the verandah looking out in the opposite direction to a sun-drenched Pangaimotu. Until, that is, the rains came again and spoilt the image.

A week after my arrival I received an invitation to what was euphemistically described as a Luncheon given by the people of Houma 'in appreciation of the award of the New Zealand 1990 Commemoration Medal to Baron Vaea of Houma.'

Vaea is one of His Majesty's Nobles and, in 1991, the Minister for Labour, Commerce, Industries and Tourism. He is now Prime Minister. Vaea's connection with New Zealand started early; he was the only Tongan to qualify as a pilot and to fly with the RNZAF in the Pacific theatre of World War II. His wife, Tuputupu, was a rollicking schoolgirl at the Church of England Diocesan School in Auckland. Together, they spent a period in the 1970s in London where Vaea was Tonga's first High Commissioner. Their daughter, Nanasi, is married to the King's third son, Lavaka 'Ulukalala Ata.

Born in 1921, Albert Tupou, as he was then known, flew Catalinas with No. 6 New Zealand Squadron based at Tulagi in the Solomon Islands in 1943–4. When only twenty-one, he was appointed by his Queen to the noble title of Vaea; and, in the Tongan way as well as the British on elevation to the peerage, took on his new name exclusively – except, that is, in the RNZAF. When he attended a squadron reunion in New Zealand a year or so ago, he was still plain Albert to his former Kiwi comrades in arms.

The so-called Luncheon turned out to be a feast of gargantuan proportions with hundreds of guests and participants and some brilliantly costumed dancers and songs. The *ma'ulu'ulu* and *tau'olunga* which I had not seen for so long lifted my scalp off with the grace and exuberance of the dancers.

There was one snag. I have come to the conclusion that the main difference between an ageing Tongan and an ageing *papalangi* is that the Tongan can still sit cross-legged with ease before the raised *polas* of food at a great feast; whereas the *papalangi* cannot begin to attempt it, even with difficulty. The best I could manage at Houma was to curl my left leg at an ugly angle before the right thigh and put my right leg straight out in front. The stability of the whole perilous enterprise was dependent upon a cantilevered left arm, palm downwards, behind. And as I had ruptured my left shoulder in a fall in wintry England a month before, even that support was unreliable. Anyhow, it effectively eliminated the left hand from participation in the business at hand: tucking into the array of food before us. Muslims would have approved, but there weren't any in evidence.

The Crown Prince, seated comfortably just beyond the British High Commissioner on my right, observed my predicament and uttered mischievous sounds of pseudo-sympathy.

All I could think of in response was: 'One thing that Tonga apparently still does pre-eminently well on occasions such as this is to sort out the Tongan sheep from the *papalangi* goats.'

'Yes,' said His Royal Highness, after a brief pause for reflection. 'I don't see any good reason to disagree with that.'

10

'All Dat Meat and No Potatoes'

In the Tonga of the early 1950s, the only regular means, fast or slow, of sending mail to the outside world was the occasion of the four-weekly call at Nuku'alofa by the Union Steam Ship Company's *Tofua*. True, when there were sufficient extra bananas to ship, the same company's *Matua* would call; and there was an infrequent Bank Line freighter to load copra. Three or four times a year, an RNZAF Sunderland, on what was called an operations training flight from Laucala Bay in Fiji, would put down in a cascade of spray on Nuku-'alofa harbour.

The *Tofua* came in at seven o'clock every fourth Monday morning. This was Mail Day, a known calendar-ringed date, quite distinct from the other fortuitous opportunities. There were a few hectic hours when commercial firms, government departments (well, some government departments), Church missions and countless families all waited impatiently for their accumulated stack of inward mail. Passions ran high and complaints were legion whenever there was delay in the sorting room. Incoming correspondence was wanted at the earliest moment, if it was to be dealt with and the replies lodged in the Post Office by the following day's deadline for the closure of the outward mail bags in that telexless and faxless world.

In those years, Air New Zealand was known as Tasman Empire Airways Limited. TEAL had inaugurated what was promoted as the Coral Route – Auckland, Suva, Apia, Aitutaki, Papeete and back. They thus linked New Zealand, Fiji, Western Samoa, the Cook Islands and Tahiti, but not Tonga – a significant omission, its government thought, from this pioneering Polynesian air journey. The aircraft used was the Solent flying-boat, comfortable and roomy, with an upper passenger deck long before Boeing thought of it for their huge 747.

Official approaches to TEAL – that Tonga be included as a Coral Route scheduled stop – were to no avail. Circumnavigationally, it was off direct routing. For this purpose, Maui Kisikisi and Maui 'Atalanga had thus misplaced the location of Tonga's emergence from the depths of the Pacific Ocean and the potential passenger traffic and cargo would not, commercially, justify a side-service. The

Solent could carry about forty-eight passengers: twelve per engine. It was unarguable that the financial break-even point would not be reached, especially since few Tongans could afford the expected fares.

But nevertheless there was the need for a regular scheduled airmail service. Spurred on by the Premier, Prince Tungi, the Government entered into negotiations with TEAL for a charter service from Suva to Nuku'alofa. It was all of 420 miles. Agreement was eventually reached under which the Government of Tonga would initially pay TEAL the princely sum of £125 per flying hour. In return, the Government would obtain a 'free' inward and outward airmail service thirteen times a year; and its coffers would be enhanced by passenger traffic receipts. Supposedly.

Great was the anticipatory public excitement, I can tell you, as the date of the inaugural flight to the Kingdom drew close in 1954. There were to be elaborate festivities and ceremonies of welcome by the Premier and Ministers of the Government to the General Manager of TEAL, his senior directors, an adventurous journalist or two, and Captain Joe Shepherd and his Solent crew.

The omens were fair in the morning. The weather was benign and the harbour calm for the landing. The Superintendent of Telegraphs and Telephones, headphones clamped to his ears, was in the back of his Ford pick-up to advise the aircraft captain that the wind was south-east at five knots; the sky was clear; there were no fishing boats in the flight path for landing; and, so far as he could see from the shore, no one was swimming where he shouldn't be. Furthermore, the Customs launch, recovered from its recent mechanical malingering, was fit and well and would be in attendance with the ropes for the buoys.

'Special day,' said Joe Shepherd when he heard this. 'All mod cons down there.'

An hour after the landing had been safely accomplished and the distinguished visitors had been brought ashore to songs, dances and flowers, they all sat down amid royal rusticity to a lavish feast. The Premier welcomed the guests. He extolled a great day in the development of external communications for Tonga. Its significance and benefits could not be overstated. On behalf of the Government of Tonga and all its people, he expressed appreciation for the pioneering enterprise and efficiency of TEAL which had brought this day about. He was confident that it was but the beginning of a longlasting and fruitful association with the airline.

Geoffrey Roberts, TEAL's General Manager in those days, replied

in reverse. He praised the foresight and enterprise of the Premier and
Government of Tonga, committed his airline to serving the interests
of its people and, flushed with the richness of Tongan feasting, drinking and dancing, said that, sadly, they must begin to leave, if they
were to get down on the waters of Laucala Bay in Fiji before darkness
fell and he was to make peace with his wife. It had been a great
inaugural, one he would never forget.

He was right. But for the wrong reasons. As he rose from the
still-groaning *polas*, the Premier beckoned to me and asked: 'Have
you seen the mail?'

'No,' I said. 'Now that you mention it. No, I haven't. Odd, that.
I'll ask.' And in what used to be described as *sotto voce*, I turned to
our new partners in progress and said, 'Just a small question, Geoff,
before you depart.'

'Sure,' he replied. 'Ask me. Anything. Absolutely anything. It's
been great.'

'It's just the minor matter of the mail? Was it . . . ah . . . brought
ashore?'

Well, you know that old nursery song about the king who wanted
butter for his bread? First he asked the queen and the queen asked
the butler and the butler asked the cook and the cook asked the
parlour maid and the parlour maid asked the dairy maid and the
dairy maid . . .

'Joe,' said the General Manager to his chief pilot. 'Where's the
mail?'

'I don't know,' replied Joe agreeably. 'I just fly the thing, remember. I suppose it's . . . somewhere. I'll ask the Second Officer.'

'Where's the Royal Tongan Mail?' he hissed down the line to the
assembled flight deck and cabin crew.

The blank New Zealand faces may have been red, but they were
still blank. A finger-tapping General Manager waited.

There was what is generally known as a pregnant pause; then a
hesitant observation from the navigator: 'I don't think we loaded it
– if that was what was in those canvas sacks I saw on the jetty at
Laucala Bay. Nobody told me about mail and anyway, I just . . .'

'. . . navigate the bloody thing,' said the chief pilot. 'And we
haven't got a manifest for Tongan mail yet, I suppose?' He glared at
the purser.

They turned to their General Manager who rose slowly to his feet.
The word is apoplectic, I think.

'It would seem, Mr Premier, that I have no alternative but to
offer to you and to the Government and people of Tonga my most

profound personal apologies and that of Tasman Empire Airways. For reasons not yet fully clear, we appear to have shortloaded your mail. That this should happen on this day of days is beyond my comprehension. But you have my personal assurance that it will never happen again.'

Prince Tungi smiled. 'I am sure it won't – not if the charter contract is terminated by the Government.'

The goodbyes were a bit stilted. Back in my office, I drew up the headings for a sort of outline cost-benefit analysis of Day One of the new commercial/airmail charter service:

RECEIPTS		EXPENSES (to be costed)
Paying Passengers	nil	Five flying hours at £125 per hour
Freight	nil	Air Traffic Control
Incoming Mail	nil	Communications
Miscellaneous	nil	Customs
		Immigration
		Police
		Medical
		Launch and crew
		Harbour sweeping (before landing and take-off)
		Publicity and printing
		Transport for guests
		Feast, garlands and gifts
		General entertainment and hospitality
TOTAL	NIL	

All in all, it had been a good day really. In a Tongan kind of way. Notwithstanding the mail menopause.

11

More Diversions of a Government Secretary

The Secretary to the Government was responsible to the Premier for the day-to-day administration of the public service. He still is, but the title of the expanded post is now Chief Secretary and Secretary to the Cabinet.

Right, I thought, early on in 1953. Let's find out who is where: what the establishment is in each ministry and department; and the salary scales, individual salaries, dates of appointment, promotion, and so on. Seemingly basic stuff.

No one could tell me. True, the Treasury had a monthly salary list and it was reasonable to suppose that those payments were correct (in Nuku'alofa at least) because a salaries clerk went round the offices at the end of each month and paid our salaries in Government of Tonga bank notes which he produced from an ageing attaché case. These were solemnly counted out by the pay clerk and handed over to the recipient who counted them again and signed the salaries sheet as having received the correct amount.

Well, correct in the sense that he confirmed that he received what he was given and what he was accustomed to expect. If it was short, he complained. If it was more, he remained silent. But no one seemed to know with certainty whether the amounts listed beside each official name were what they should be. And incremental progression was haphazard.

I called for the departmental establishment staff lists. There were none. I asked for the Civil Service staff list. There was none. I asked for the list of weekly paid non-established workers. Same answer. I questioned some of the salary scales. They did not all reconcile with those shown in the annual estimates of expenditure approved by the Legislative Assembly. Differences were said to have been approved in some instances by Cabinet, extra-agenda and post-parliamentary budget approval, as a consequence of hard luck stories or special pleas from close ministerial relatives.

Then I discovered that the files were thick with unanswered complaints about alleged short-changing by the Treasury. Worse still was the day when a telegram arrived from the remote and at that time isolated northern island of Niuatoputapu. Its sole link with the rest of Tonga was a three-monthly ketch of erratic reliability and scheduling, apart that is from the wireless transmission of a solitary key-tapping telegraphist.

The office messenger slipped the telegram on to my desk and departed. He offered no comment and no advice as to what I should do. Unusual, I thought, as I looked at what he had brought.

To: THE SECRETARY TO GOVERNMENT
            PREMIER'S OFFICE
            NUKU'ALOFA.
From: THE WIRELESS OPERATOR, CLASS II,
            NIUATOPUTAPU
Subject: SALARY

Sir,

I do not wish to trouble you, but I cannot keep silent any longer and I have to think of buying food this week as my coconuts are finished and I have three children and Quensell's store will not give me any more credit. They say they are fed up with me, Sir.

I was posted to Niua as your wireless man three years ago and since then I have always carried out my duties and never missed a sked★ with Nuku'alofa. Often I have been wet and cold and sick, yet I have never complained.

I now humbly draw Your Honour's attention to the fact that for all this time I have not yet received any salary from the Government. I have not asked before because I do not want to be nuisance.

I know you are very busy serving the ministers and do not have much time to feed a small hungry sea bird singing to you from the other side of the big lagoon. But please, Sir, would you investigate to see if someone has slipped up as it will soon be Christmas.

I respectfully await your decision.

Your faithful wireless man at Niua.

★Daily scheduled times for transmission and reception of telegrams.

I called for the departmental files. His appointment and posting were there all right. But that was it. The file had been put away. The Treasury had not been notified to pay him and his department had not been sent a copy of the details.

He received a handsome apology, warm appreciation of his dedicated loyalty and, with the agreement of a somewhat begrudging Treasurer, three years' back pay with interest and an appropriate bonus. The singing of the hungry sea bird from across the lagoon had at last been heard.

In such circumstances, it took two years for a first complete staff list of the Tonga Civil Service to be put together, typed, printed, bound and distributed with appointments, classifications, gradings, salary scales and salaries. It also included ministers of the Crown, members of the Legislative Assembly and of government-appointed boards and committees. It was a Tongan first in one respect at least – that some sort of basic staff management began to be possible. There were, however, other more intransigent problems and they were not confined to Tongan members of the Civil Service.

There was the case of the tenacious Mr Blanchflower. He was a surveyor nearing the end of his career, seconded under contract to the Government of Tonga from the British overseas surveys service as executive head of the Lands and Survey Department in Nuku-'alofa. He worked just across the road (conveniently so, as it turned out) from the Premier's office. It was there I sat, just through the wall from the Cabinet room of Prince Tungi.

One day my incoming correspondence folder included a brief letter from Mr Blanchflower, submitted through his minister who initialled and passed it on without comment. The minister was Prince Tu'ipelehake, the younger brother of the Premier.

As you know [the letter said], I shall shortly be proceeding on end of contract leave. I am entitled to free passages to the United Kingdom for myself and my family and to six months' paid leave.

As I plan to remain in New Zealand for some time, I shall be grateful if you will authorise the Treasury to pay me before I leave the Kingdom

(a) the monetary provision for the foregone New Zealand–United Kingdom passages, and

(b) my leave salary in one lump sum.

I said 'no' to both requests, explained why and put the file away.

Not so Mr Blanchflower. A week later, the Acting Premier called me in to see him. Tungi was in the course of one of his absences on overseas duty. The Deputy Premier, Havea Tu'iha'ateiho, was on leave. 'Ulukalala Ata, my dual personality Minister of Police and

Prisons, was sitting in the Premier's chair and enjoying every minute of it.

'Mr Blanchflower,' he said, 'has been to see me and lodged an official appeal against your decision on his leave requests. I shall have to consider it.'

'Very well,' I said, 'I'll put the papers to you.' And did so. I explained in a detailed minute that the passage entitlement was not a monetary one and that if a passage was foregone it could not be transubstantiated into a financial benefit. Anyway there was provision in the contract, as Mr Blanchflower well knew, for the passage entitlement to be held good for a period of twelve months which ought to be enough for him to decide whether he would return to the United Kingdom or remain settled in New Zealand. On the leave salary point I said that leave pay was just like ordinary pay. It accrued and was payable as it was earned. There was no lump-sum advance eligibility.

That, I thought, would be that.

It wasn't.

'Mr Blanchflower has been to see me again,' said the Acting Premier, a week later. 'I explained to him what you said. He is not very happy.'

'But what do you consider is the correct answer to him?' I asked. There was a long pause.

'I am not very happy either. We have to think about our relations with the United Kingdom. It might not be good for Tonga if we are too hard on him.'

'I am not, with respect, being hard at all. It is a matter of adhering to the rules and accepted contractual and personnel practices. I believe I have done so.'

'I think,' said 'Ulukalala, unmoved, 'that we should ask Cabinet what it thinks and let Cabinet decide.'

After a further period of debate, I accepted defeat and went off to prepare a Cabinet submission. I set out the potential hazards of an ill-judged decision and asked if I could be in attendance at the meeting. 'Seeking to exercise improper influence on the Tongan ministers', this was later called by one Cabinet member.

It seemed sensible also to ask the Treasury to calculate the likely annual cost of internal passage eligibility foregone by Tongan civil servants, dozens of whom never used them; some antipodean expatriates and Tongans who could become eligible for paid passages to the United Kingdom after long service and often didn't take them; and whether anyone – Tongan or European – had ever been paid all accrued leave salary entitlement in a lump sum on departure from the Civil Service and Tonga. Answer: none – and rightly, said a taciturn Treasurer. As he was a member of the Cabinet, the outcome seemed assured. If it wasn't, personnel administrative mayhem would be let loose.

The Cabinet spent two hours on the case one morning. Blanchflower had done some effective lobbying. The Treasurer was obdurate; but the fear of incurring the supposed wrath of the British Government, which still had fading residual responsibilities for Tonga at that time, made some ministers uneasy. So, unbelievably, they referred the matter for consideration by the Privy Council over which, once a week, the Queen presided. The absence of the Premier had perhaps been felt.

Meanwhile Blanchflower hied himself off to the British Agent and Consul and poured out his woes. These were duly relayed back to the Palace in good time before the expected day of judgment. By then, the argument was public knowledge; attitudes were being taken for and against; the Civil Service buzzed with conjectural curiosity; and in the Legislative Assembly, a Representative of the People warned that it just proved what he had always said – that 'the minister should send all the Europeans home and leave our Tongan boys to run the Government in accordance with the Constitution without foreign interference . . .'

The Privy Council delivered a delphic judgment.

'Decision to be left to the Acting Premier and Secretary to the Government.'

Thanks very much, I thought. They are not Polynesians for nothing. What next? I drafted a long letter for signature this time by the Acting Premier. I accompanied it with an even more detailed argument and analysis of the implications for the Civil Service if the Blanchflower manoeuvres were successful. After 'Ulukalala had read it, I spent forty-five minutes with him going through the whole thing to ensure that it was all understood and that, hopefully, realism would prevail.

'Ulukalala listened attentively throughout and said not a word. When I had finished, he reached for his pen, signed the letter and placed an impressive official seal over his signature.

That, I thought, is that. Now I can get back to some proper work. I called a messenger and had the letter hand-delivered across the road. Blanchflower was leaving next day.

Nothing is certain – for long – in Tonga. That afternoon I heard a familiar and very loud voice through the masonry partition from the Premier's office. Ten minutes later, 'Ulukalala called me in.

'You know that letter that was sent to Mr Blanchflower?'

Did I not. 'Yes, of course,' I said, with mounting unease.

'He has just been to see me. He is very angry. He is threatening to take up the matter with the Secretary of State in London. I want another letter to go to him today agreeing to his requests.'

I looked out of the window and took what is normally known as a deep breath.

'Can you please tell me why?'

'I think . . . Well, I think that is what you should do. I do not want Tonga to be seen in a bad light.'

'What *I* should do? You will remember, Premier, my lengthy minute to you and my long and detailed explanation this morning. You agreed to this course of action then. What has happened to cause you to change your mind now?'

'I did not agree with you then,' the Premier replied.

'But you must have done. You signed the letter to Mr Blanchflower. How could you sign it if you had any doubts about it?'

He looked at me in astonishment. He was the Minister of Police and Prisons again.

'It was your letter, not mine. I signed it because you advised me to. It was my duty to sign it as Acting Premier. That is why I signed it. Just because I signed it does not mean that I agreed with what was in it. I have told Mr Blanchflower so. Now I want a different letter to go. I have made up my mind.'

He was unbudgeable. So I did as I was bidden. The Acting Premier signed that one too, the file being duly noted. 'In accordance with your oral instructions to me at four p.m. this afternoon . . .'

The *Tofua* came in next morning. Blanchflower passed me on his way to the Treasury. He gave me a Mona Lisa smile. 'I'm off now. Toodleloo, my dear chap. Have fun!'

I don't know quite why it was, but the recruitment of expatriate teachers to the Department of Education, and the problems they created once in post, occupied over half my available time for the administration of the Tonga Civil Service. I came to the eccentric conclusion one day that those imported from New Zealand had about the same emotional and intellectual range as some of their more juvenile pupils, which might have accounted for their supposed capacity to relate to twelve-year-olds day after day.

There was what was called a Scheme of Co-operation with the

New Zealand Department of Education in Wellington for finding teachers prepared to go on loan to the governments of Fiji, Samoa, Niue, the Cook Islands and Tonga. It was a laborious and sometimes unsuccessful process, but no better option was available.

Tonga College at 'Atele was the pride and joy of the Government and the focus of its efforts was to provide middle-school agricultural education for boys. It had adequate buildings, splendid grounds, an imaginative curriculum, lots of practical work, the best school brass band in the Kingdom – but no headmaster. Not, anyway, for over three years. Staff morale had disintegrated and discipline had grown lax. Then at long last the Officer for Islands Education in Wellington found a New Zealand teacher of modest attainments who, with his Cook Islands wife, was willing to come to Tonga for two years, subject to his being satisfied on arrival with his living quarters. Curious, I thought, and a bit ominous as I sent a cable of concurrence in the *faute de mieux* appointment.

Monday morning, twelve weeks later, the *Tofua* sailed into Nuku'alofa harbour from Auckland and Suva. By seven a.m. Vuna wharf was ablaze with red and white uniforms as the entire college enrolment lined both sides. The band pounded out Tongan welcome music and the staff paraded below the ship's gangway to get a first glimpse of the New Man. The long leadership drought was at an end. Or so we thought.

English and Tongan speeches of welcome united Tonga, New Zealand and the Cook Islands in a golden educational future. There were flower presentations, interminable hand shakes, great bowls of *kava*, school songs and massed dances, all on the small wharf. Twenty cases of personal effects came ashore amid the monthly confusion of cargo discharge, passenger disembarkation, a huge mail consignment, plus overloaded trucks with hundreds of banana boxes for shipment and general cargo to bring ashore. It was all helped merrily along by the fact that the Customs gave in early, watching it all and 'waiving' it through, while Immigration thoughtfully stayed away altogether. A really good Friendly Islands occasion: relaxed officialdom and general goodwill. This will impress him, I thought.

Next morning all had changed. A frantic Director of Education sought me out, accompanied by the new Headmaster of Tonga College.

'I have to tell you,' he said without preamble, 'that I am leaving this afternoon on the *Tofua* to return to New Zealand. My wife cannot stand rats and there were rats in the roof of the house at

'Atele. She was terrified and hysterical all night. She refuses to stay. If she goes, I go too. I lost one wife because of cockroaches in Samoa and I'm not going to lose another because of rats in Tonga. That's why she left the Cook Islands in the first place.'

I looked at the Director of Education. 'But didn't the staff and boys spend about a month sprucing up the house and putting in new furniture and mosquito nets and all that? Surely what I might call rodent extermination . . .'

'Yes, and I'm grateful for that,' said the retiring Headmaster of Tonga College. 'But it's not the point. No rodents were exterminated, it would seem. If I don't go this afternoon, I'm stuck here for four weeks. So I'm leaving today.'

We spent another half an hour to no purpose and I gave in.

'There will be the small matter of refund of inward passage and other expenses,' I said. 'Your contract is explicit.'

'But it is not explicit about rats in our bedroom, so I shall not pay. Goodbye. I have to get all my boxes back to the ship. And I shall be claiming back my return passage costs because of deliberate misrepresentation of contract terms.'

There followed what is known as a precipitate departure. I dictated a cable to Wellington.

That afternoon at three p.m. he and his wife went back up the ship's gangway. This time there was no one at the wharf when the *Tofua* sailed north to Vava'u an hour later. Tonga College relapsed into numbed mourning. Classes were abandoned for the rest of the week and the bandmaster cancelled all rehearsals and performances. No one had the stomach to play.

So ended that twenty-four-hour appointment. He must be some sort of Guinness record, I thought. As well as the time, energy and money spent on the fruitless filling – and unfilling – of one teaching post in Tonga. It was eighteen months before the personal file was put away and twelve more before another appointment was made. This time the welcome ceremonies were neither so elaborate nor so fervent.

12

Legendary Interlude: How Fire Came Into The World

Maui Kisikisi and his brother Maui 'Atalanga lived in the chiefly spirit land of Pulotu. When they worked in the fields, they enjoyed succulent food cooked for them by old Maui, their father. And if you remember their arduous search for the daughter of Tongamata-moana, you will know how much they cared for good food.

From time to time, they returned to the earth world to weed the grasses and clean the jungles. But in the earth world they had to eat their food raw and uncooked since there was no fire there.

Old Maui – or Maui Motu'a as he is called in the Tongan language – kept the secret of fire from his sons because he suspected that they would want to take fire to the earth world. So he did not let his sons observe how he prepared their food.

When they worked together in Pulotu, Maui Motu'a would say, 'Do not slacken in your hoeing, my sons. I am going now to cook for you. Pray do not look back at me or at the ground we have already hoed; for if you do, evil will befall us all.'

Long tantalised by the delicious smell of his father's cooking and impatient of his prohibition, Maui Kisikisi found himself one day unable to resist the temptation to look back where his father was cooking in a part of the garden which they had hoed that morning. He straightened up, gazed behind him and then bent down to go on with his work. And so he saw fire for the first time.

When their hoeing was finished, Maui Motu'a said: 'You have laboured enough today. Let us stop now and we shall eat the food I have prepared.'

When they stood up to go, Maui Motu'a and Maui 'Atalanga and Maui Kisikisi saw that the place which they had cleared with their hoes was now overgrown again with weeds.

Maui Motu'a became very angry. 'Which of you,' he asked in a terrible voice, 'looked back at me while I was cooking our food?'

'Father, it was I,' admitted Maui Kisikisi, and bowed his head in shame before his father's displeasure.

'See what has come of your disobedience,' said Maui Motu'a. 'All the weeds we hoed have grown again. If you had obeyed me this would not have happened; and we should never have had to do our work more than once. But from now on, both here and in the earth world, we shall have to weed and weed without respite; and so will all who come after us. Since I am old, it will be no great punishment for me. As for you, come and eat and then go back to your everlasting labour in the earth world.'

So they ate in silence. Maui Kisikisi pondered his father's words and grew angry that he had not been warned of the consequences of disobeying his father. He determined to be revenged on Maui Motu'a by carrying the fire of Pulotu to the earth world and thus be able to have cooked food whenever they wanted to work there.

When their meal was over, Maui Kisikisi slipped away to the place where his father had prepared the meal. He picked up a hot stone in the cleft of a stick and, holding it behind his back, he joined his father and brother for their journey to the earth world.

Silently Maui Kisikisi placed the stone against the tail end of the girdle of *tapa* that his father was wearing. Soon it started to smoulder without the old man being aware of it. But as they emerged above the surface of the ground, Maui Motu'a noticed the smell of burning *tapa* cloth.

Looking down, he saw that it was his own girdle that was on fire. Turning to his son, he shouted: 'Wretched boy, look what you have done now!'

As he cried out, he tried to extinguish the fire, but Maui Kisikisi shouted: 'Run away, fire, run away to the *fukofuka* tree and all the other trees of the earth. Run away and multiply so that you can never be held captive again.'

When Maui Motu'a succeeded in putting out the fire on his girdle, it was too late to do anything else. The fire had already gone to live, quiet and unseen, in the trees of the world, never to be captured again.

And this is how fire first came to the earth; and this is why it is that, although friction can bring fire from any kind of dry wood, it comes most easily from the wood of the *fukofuka* tree. For it was such a tree that grew beside the entrance to the spirit land of Pulotu.

There is today a young elected Representative of the People in the Tonga Legislative Assembly. His name is Viliami Fukofuka and he is also President of the Tonga National Youth Congress. I wonder if his popular support will spread like that early fire in the world.

PART TWO

You preserve traditions only by keeping them up to date.

Lord Whitelaw, 1987

13

A Testing Time

'What,' asked 'Eseta, 'do you think is the essential difference between Tonga and everywhere else? There's the examination question. You've come here to look us over. You answer it.'

'OK,' I said. 'Here goes. The difference between Tonga and the rest of the perceived world is this: on the one hand, the Tonga Government does some strange things that most other governments would not dream of doing; on the other, it contrives not to get involved in serious issues which cause other countries to jump up and down with excitement or alarm. This is why Tongans make desirable chairmen of Commonwealth or other international gatherings. There are two reasons. One: they always know when it is time to adjourn for coffee. And two: they can never be charged with being biased – except about themselves – because they never (well, hardly ever) hold extreme views about anything except the undesirability of holding extreme views. I'll give you two examples.

'The Crown Prince, representing his uncle, the Prime Minister, at a Commonwealth heads of government meeting was once assailed during an interval for corridor lobbying. He was asked what the views of the Government of Tonga were about a regular burning issue on the agenda and one which, as usual, was dividing prime ministers and presidents more than somewhat.

'"Views!" His Royal Highness replied. "We have opinions, yes. But I think it would be more courteous if we kept those to ourselves. We don't have to express views on everything that comes up, do we? What a boring life it would be if we were all so conformist. I thought that was what the Commonwealth was supposed to be all about – strength from diversity, or something like that. So if we were to give our views on anything on this agenda, it would be on the side of diversity."

'As you know, 'Eseta, everything takes its character and style from the top: be it a family, a business, a government or a monarchy. You will remember that a decade or so ago 'Inoke Faletau, now Director of the Commonwealth Foundation, was High Commissioner for Tonga in London. It was the turn of the South Pacific to find someone to be chairman for a year of the Board of Directors of the Commonwealth Fund for Technical Cooperation. The nod went to Tonga and to its High Commissioner who was not, he confessed, overly preoccupied in London with Tonga's state affairs.

'The occasional meetings of the Board at Marlborough House offered moments of fun and genial high jinks for the chairman of the day. He could mercifully find light relief at serious moments and could rarely see anything on the agenda to get steamed up about. Should Nigeria and India lock antagonistic horns on some passing question, 'Inoke would turn on rays of instant Tongan sunshine amid a bleak English winter and all would somehow be well.

'As I arrived for one such meeting at a Bahamas hotel in the early 1980s, I was startled by a great shout of "Ken!" The source of this unexpectedly penetrating greeting was not immediately apparent. I finally located it as coming from a rotund Polynesian torso resting contentedly nearby in the warm Caribbean waters off the Nassau beach.

"Come on in," he said. "As you can see, I am preparing for our meeting in the Tongan way. The agenda is too absurdly mundane to be taken seriously . . ."

'So if I could have a magic wand,' I said to 'Eseta, 'I would appoint only Tongans to umpire all cricket test matches and only Tongans to referee all international rugby union matches – except for those between Tonga and Fiji.'

'Have you finished?' asked 'Eseta.

'Yes, I suppose I have. Did I pass?'

'I guess so. Do you want to hear the examiner's report?'

'I'm not sure.'

'Well, you're going to anyway.'

She smiled and went on in that richly resonant contralto voice of hers. 'I liked the bit at the beginning about what we do and don't do. That was pleasantly perceptive. But take my advice and don't run on so. You are in danger of becoming too ruminative in your old age. If you are going to make a serious attempt at writing about the new Tongans, get some facts into the pipeline. Nitty-gritty stuff. Go and look at the graffiti on the transverse of the *Ha'amonga*. Then read the Estimates. Here they are.'

'Good idea,' I said. 'Shall I do you first? The Tongan woman today. The feminine revolution sort of thing?'

'Nonsense,' she said. 'You know better than that. Tonga has

always been a predominantly matriarchal society. We never needed women's lib and don't need to be patronised now.'

'All right, all right,' I said. 'Just an idea. I've lost interest in it already.'

'A recent UNESCO study,' she went on relentlessly, 'says that more than five hundred million illiterate women live in the rural regions of Third World countries. It does not say, but I can, that there is not a single illiterate woman in the whole of Tonga. You may not want me to drive the point home, but I will: our women are the future of the New Friendly Islands.'

I thought not of Tonga but of Togo whither some of my personal correspondence used to vanish without trace. (One or two of my letters turned up later stamped 'Not Togo – try Tonga.') 'All this was curious,' I said to 'Eseta, 'since the illiteracy rate in Togo among women is apparently about seventy per cent.'

'That sort of interpolation,' said 'Eseta severely, 'does not do you justice. You are avoiding or evading – whatever word the tax people use – the real issue. Here, now, as things are, is what you should be writing about. That's what I thought you intended to do.'

'I'll continue to try,' I said without much conviction. 'But it seems to be getting harder and harder.'

'And while it may not be a matter of current concern to you,' said 'Eseta with an air of finality, 'I've just heard on the BBC news from Radio Tonga that it is snowing heavily in Kent and that temperatures are well below zero and are expected to fall further.'

There didn't seem to be any answer to that. Not coming from the Government's Information Officer.

14

Waiting for the Coconuts to Fall

The Legislative Assembly Building in Nuku'alofa has a relaxing old-world atmosphere. You could mistake it for a late nineteenth-century South Pacific wooden church. Rectangular in shape, it has a white-painted exterior and high white concave ceiling. The flag of Tonga – scarlet with a white quarter bearing a red cross – flies above the entrance doorway when the Assembly is sitting. Stained-glass windows are set to left and right at the front. Blue drapes adorn the side windows. Outsize naked light bulbs dangle well below ineffectual circular shades at just the height, seemingly, to hit members' heads when they stand to speak. Microphone stands and small wooden speakers clutter the horse-shoe of members' desks. Smoking is permitted before sessions start and during intervals. The deep-brown-stained walls are lined with the fading photographs of past Assembly members, watching no doubt in critical appraisal of the performance of their successors today.

There are thirty-three landed estates of the nobility in Tonga, and the incumbents of these, which include most of the ministers, elect their representatives every three years. At the same time the 'people' do likewise – all literate Tongans, other than nobles, who pay taxes and are over the age of twenty-one being eligible to vote. The Assembly thus virtually consists of a joint Upper and Lower House.

Since the Representatives of the People have been known to vote *en bloc* against the Government bench, the nobles hold the balance of power. Normally they vote with the Government, but sometimes a few do not. It does not seem to matter.

'Apart from the possible exception of Switzerland,' the King once remarked, 'Tonga is, I believe, the only country in the world where a responsible Government is in a perpetual minority in the Legislature; but it has comfort in the knowledge that even if it is outvoted on a material point it does not go out of office!'

The reason is that the ministers, although constitutionally responsible, are appointed during the pleasure of the Sovereign, as is the Speaker. They are not politicians in the sense understood elsewhere. Since they are often chiefs in their own right, the authority of a written constitution is reinforced by the traditions of a thousand years of Tongan life where rank is authority and ultimate authority has customary rank.

So out of a total of thirty members, twelve of the Assembly are appointed by the Sovereign; nine members are elected by and from among thirty-three nobles; and only nine members are actually elected by popular vote. As things stand, it is clear that those nine Representatives of the People, voting together, can never win when opposed by the combined forces of sovereign-appointed and nobles-elected members. And thereby hangs a tale to which I shall return.

The Speaker's chair stands on a raised dais behind which are two great flags in Tongan red and white and the official coat of arms. '*'Eiki Sea*,' it says on the name plate before Noble Fusitu'a, recently appointed by the King to be Speaker and husband of my examiner on things Tongan, 'Eseta Fusitu'a. *'Eiki* means 'chief' and *Sea* is the Tonganised version, in two syllables (say-a), of 'chair'.

The Tongan name for the Assembly is *Fale Alea* – House of Speaking or Debate. In this respect, it does not disappoint. The Assembly usually has one long annual session from about June to September. But in February 1991, it was called together exceptionally to deal with urgent legislative business of a controversial nature. Not since the aftermath of Hurricane Isaac in 1982 had such emergency action been found necessary by the Government.

At the start of a sitting, members rise and bow to the Speaker as he enters. Prayers follow; and, in rich resonant unaccompanied male voices in perfect pitch, a hymn: on this occasion the Tongan version of 'What a friend we have in Jesus'. As events were to turn out, such an assurance may have been of comfort to the official benches.

Then the roll call by the clerk. Each member rises as he is named and says '*Koau eni*' (I am here). They sink back into their huge red cloth copper-studded chairs, XOS size to fit the ample Polynesian bodies of most of the members. Most because, in general, it is the chiefs whose physique expands so noticeably in middle age and there-after. There is, with one exception, a slimmed-down look today on the benches of the Representatives of the People. Youth has taken over; sons are replacing less formally educated fathers. They carry their Australasian university degrees as lightly as their years.

The parliamentary staff who are chosen and appointed by the Assembly itself sit around an oblong table in the centre of the floor. They include clerks, shorthand writers, tape monitors, and a tech-nician from the Government radio station with his rolling tapes for selective delayed broadcast.

The chamber has no ceiling fans. Portable blowers were brought in one steaming day as ministers fanned themselves ineffectually. Jackets are mandatory when the House is in session and the Speaker presides; to great relief all round, it's 'jackets off' when the Assembly goes into a Committee of the whole House. There is no room for a public gallery. Two press men were squeezed in. I sat at the back behind the ministerial seats between 'Eseta on my left and the sergeant at arms on my right. Of forbidding mien with a close-cropped Prussian haircut, he spent most of the time getting up, bowing to the chair, passing some papers a yard or so, bowing again and resuming his seat. On one singular occasion, he rose, bowed, spat with venom through the open door beside him, bowed again and resumed his seat. I was not sure whether it was some sort of comment on the speaker at the time.

The procedures of the Tonga Legislative Assembly are said to follow those of Westminster. Members regularly participate in the affairs of the Commonwealth Parliamentary Association. But the parallels cannot be stretched too far. Free-flow oratory takes priority. The proceedings are exclusively in the Tongan language with its layers of linguistic and customary constraints according to rank and status: three languages in one in fact, one to address the King, one to address the nobles and one for everyday or domestic 'commoner' usage. And the vocabulary is quite distinct in each case.

I made an intriguing discovery. The debates inside the House in February 1991 became tense and quasi-confrontational at one stage. During a break, members carried on the debate in groups of four or five on the lawns outside the chamber; Ministers and Representatives of both Nobles and People mingled together and argued with controlled forcefulness. In each group, they spoke in English. Scarcely a word of Tongan.

I sought expert advice as to why this was. 'It is very simple really,' I was told. 'English is a great equaliser, a leveller. Members can more or less forget differences in rank, status and seniority by speaking English. Not so of course when they use Tongan.'

Simple indeed once you know. Like everything in life, nothing is more obvious than a mystery explained for the benefit of the ignorant. Why couldn't I have figured that out for myself? But I suppose there may be a further point: in the 1950s many of the older members were less well equipped in the English language. The use of English then would have been for my benefit, not theirs.

So the Lords of Tonga sit jointly with, but separated from, the commoners in the Legislative Assembly. This is, of course, unlike parliamentary practice at Westminster in London. There the privileged upper chamber only permits the elected members of the lower chamber to enter its gilt-decorated splendour to hear the Queen's Speech and then only when they have been bidden by three loud raps of a black rod on their door. The man who wields it is in fact called Black Rod. It is not only the Tongans, we have to conclude, who have traditional practices which are mysteries to the uninitiated or to the culturally unenlightened.

On Tuesday 21 January 1992, a debate took place in the House of Lords on an unusual subject. At 8.03 p.m., Lord Glenarthur, who may or may not have been talking to Tonga's royal Minister for Foreign Affairs, rose to ask Her Majesty's Government, 'what is their policy towards the island states of the South Pacific . . . My reason for [asking] is not, I hasten to say, because I doubt that Her Majesty's Government have a policy towards the island states of the South Pacific. I most certainly know that they have . . .'

Well, I thought, when I saw the Hansard account of the debate, let us see what enlightenment lies within. Not all that much, as it turned out. Lord Glenarthur roamed over military coups in Fiji, the South Pacific Commission, French nuclear testing, the South Pacific Forum, the British position in respect of the Treaty of Rarotonga concerning a nuclear-free zone in the South Pacific and, a final vanity, 'the enthusiasm which the island states [of the region] show for our continued interest'.

Lord Auckland resurrected memories of Queen Salote's ride in the rain and the memorable occasion on which British and Tongan choirs sang carols on a Christmas Day broadcast of *Songs of Praise*.

Baroness Ewart-Biggs (the widow of the British Ambassador murdered in 1976 by the IRA in Dublin) asked some penetrating and apposite questions about British aid to Fiji and the ethical basis for the continued training by Britain of Fijian armed forces. She elicited no real answer. It was one of her last speaking appearances as a Labour peer in the House of Lords. Eight months later, aged sixty-three, she was to die of cancer.

The Earl of Caithness replied on behalf of the Government. His statement was laced with the high-flown sentiments of civil service drafting, competent but largely meaningless.

'We intend to continue to maintain our interest and involvement in the [South Pacific] region. We will go on doing our bit to promote sustainable economic and social development. We will continue to seek to encourage regional co-operation among island states as a source of strength and as the best means to pursue their common interests. And we will keep up our contribution to the promotion of good government in the region . . .'

Only five speakers filled eighteen pages of Hansard. The debate lasted an hour although no one was really much the wiser when it was over. Yet at least some of it was better said than unsaid and it is now on the record for the Polynesians, the Melanesians and the Micronesians in this vast ocean of islands to digest and to make of it what they can.

15

'Money and Time are of Little Moment'

That is what I, like Tevita Toutaiolepo, used to think too. In 1966, I wrote this:

> The Tongan has not yet learned the truth about time. It has no vital meaning for him. 'They can cope with almost anything else,' said a despairing New Zealand hospital matron, 'but they just have trouble with time.'

Well not any more they don't, if the practices of the Legislative Assembly are any guide to latter-day understanding of the new Friendly Islanders. Indeed, money and time are said by some to dominate all other considerations. In this supposedly timeless society, the clock in the chamber, not the Speaker, determines all. The daily sitting starts at ten o'clock: on time, as the clock is striking. Watches outside are co-ordinated to ensure that it is so. An hour later there is a break of fifteen minutes; then the sitting resumes until midday. Sharp. On the dot. As the last noonday chime rings out, the chamber is empty. Ditto in the afternoon between two and four. At two minutes to four, members rise and begin to prepare for departure. Whoever is speaking – Prime Minister, Minister for Foreign Affairs, Minister of Police, noble or commoner – gives up and stops. No one is paying the slightest attention to him. In seconds, it seems, the chamber is empty. All are gone, the ministers in their chauffeur-driven Mercedes and Hyundai. So a parliamentary day is effectively of three and a half hours, unless there is an evening session. Then additional considerations enter the arena.

In the 1950s, each member, including ministers, was paid a daily attendance allowance. I made no headway whatsoever in getting agreement to eliminate this open invitation to sessions (not sittings) of limitless duration by the introduction of an annual allowance. Today things are different, but not all that different. For all members, ministers included, there is an annual allowance (T$12,500 in 1991) and also a daily allowance of T$55.50. The Speaker receives a little more in both cases. Then there are rent allowances, travelling allowances at T$132 per diem, transport allowances for official car-less members and annual allowances for each Representative of Nobles and People. It is not stated whether for this purpose there is a distinction between travelling ministers and members; and whether accommodation costs have to be paid from the allowance or are met additionally.

That is not all. There is the small matter of overtime about which the approved estimates of expenditure for the Legislative Assembly are singularly silent. When the House agrees to meet in the evening, as it did on three occasions during the February 1991 session, overtime is payable on the following basis: the first two hours are treated as a full day. Every hour thereafter is treated as another full day.

The Council met from six p.m. until about nine p.m. on these three occasions for which members, including ministers, collected the equivalent of an additional six full days' allowances.

Similar payments at lower rates are paid to the House staff. No wonder they are in what are regarded as prize jobs or that nepotism thrives in the promoting of appointments thereto. If members have leave of absence to be away from the House when in session, they are regarded as being present and receive all allowances for the period, including overtime. One parliamentary sub-committee set off on an internal journey by sea. From the moment they left the wharf they were deemed, I was told, to be on overtime rates; and the members of the committee were paid accordingly on the accepted basis, irrespective of whether they went on the journey or not. When I heard this, I wondered what on earth the Government Auditor was doing. It is, or should be, a matter of no little public interest that all these allowances are deemed to be tax-free.

No one person is, of course, to blame for these examples of flagrant abuse of public power. Nor have they come about recently. There has been an evolutionary process over a long period of time. But whenever there is untrammelled opportunity in offices of state, sooner or later there will be exploitation and expansion of self-interest. Decisions will come to reflect favour and benefit for those who make them. And there is always such opportunity where there is little electoral accountability and no real public awareness as to how public money is managed and spent. 'The Legislative Assembly is a cosy club operating primarily in the interests of its members,' was one opinion offered to me.

When there is no accountability, there will be corruption. And that will not be manifest solely in terms of money.

16

The Management of Public Money

It is a bit of a coincidence, I suppose, that in 1989 I became Director
of Studies for courses in financial management in government at the
Royal Institute of Public Administration (now RIPA International)
in Bedford Square, London: a coincidence only in the sense that it is
impossible to write about Tonga, now or in the past, without mention of some of its singular approaches to money raising and money
management.

I didn't need any encouragement from 'Eseta to want to see the
latest approved Estimates of the Government of Tonga. This document, which all respectable governments produce and publish, incor-
porates the details of expected revenue and proposed expenditure
for the next financial year. The heads or votes of expenditure are
summarised in the Appropriation Bill which, when enacted by the
legislating body, provides the necessary legal authority to spend the
funds in the manner and for the purposes set out in the Estimates –
funds, that is, which have been either extracted from a patient public
or borrowed. Additionally, in the case of Tonga, are the substantial
capital sums benevolently bestowed upon it, for widely varying
reasons, by national and international benefactors from money
prised from their own unwilling tax payers or contributing governments.

The document containing the 1990–1 approved Recurrent and
Development Estimates of the Kingdom of Tonga consists, believe
it or not, of all of 380 pages. The text is in the two languages,
Tongan and English. Reading it meaningfully, as they say, is hard
going. Some think that it is meant to be. I cannot believe that
its financial obfuscations have been penetrated *in toto* by many. Its
layout and style reflects an earlier era in this century, not the end
of it. The parliamentary time spent in explanations must push up
expenditure on daily allowances for the legislators at Budget time.
Perhaps, as a consequence, they don't complain. Most of them,
that is.

Recurrent expenditure in 1990–1 was estimated to be T$48 million
and development expenditure at T$36 million. Of the latter the
greater part, as you would expect, was said to be donor or loan

funded. There were no explanatory notes to any of the estimated
revenue figures; no detailed operating expenditure 'actuals' of the
latest available year, and no summarised history of the general revenue balance. Likewise no observation or explanation was offered in
respect of an estimated revised deficit of T$4.4 million in 1989–90.
And so on. The expenditure notes (except for development projects
hopefully funded from external sources) were scanty and uninforma-
tive, and the statistical tables lean.

The Budget Statement, not incorporated in the Estimates document, remedied these deficiencies only slightly.

I sought a second opinion. The first Governor of the National
Reserve Bank of Tonga seemed the appropriate person to talk to.
He was Alan Gee, an Australian with a Tongan wife and previous
service as an adviser to the Reserve Bank of Fiji. He was caustically
critical.

'Meaningful analysis of the Estimates is impossible,' he said. 'The
Development Budget is totally inflated. It is a matter of opinion as
to what will get done. There is no proper final detailed report on the
Budget out-turn. We produce a quarterly bulletin, but only with
great difficulty because we cannot get sensible figures from the Treasury. Research takes ages.'

'And the economy?'

'Remittances from Tongans overseas hold it together. They affect
about two thirds of the population, I would estimate, urban and
rural. Without them, Tonga would undoubtedly "qualify" on economic grounds as one of the least developed countries. How long the
remittances will last is anybody's guess. Succeeding generations of
expatriate Tongans may not look so favourably on the needs of their
relations at home.'

'That is invisible exports. What about visible?'

'Watermelons are doing well: eight to nine thousand to New Zealand last year. It seems to me that anything prospers that the government has had nothing to do with.'

'How do you see the structure of Tongan society?'

'The chiefly syndrome is alive and well. Power is synonymous
with chauffeur-driven cars these days. At the occasional *fono*, the
people are still told what is expected of them. Most nobles continue
to hold the view that the people are there to do what they are told;
that they were not emancipated from slavery by King George Tupou I
in 1862 to have a share in power. It remains very much a feudal
system. The Church is, of course, of the greatest importance in
Tonga. You will have seen new churches going up all over the place.

But as the materials are imported free of duty for this purpose and the labour is provided, all this construction activity doesn't produce anything.'

Building materials for churches are not the only items that might come into Tonga free of import duties. 'We had to provide VIP cars for heads of government and others attending the recent South Pacific Forum meetings in Tonga,' the Crown Prince had told me. 'We did not have enough of our own and we did not want to buy a whole array of expensive vehicles for ten days' use. So we said that they could be imported free of duty and port and Customs service tax and then be sold afterwards. That's the only way I could afford a BMW.'

It is usually contended that expenditure on Defence has special considerations of confidentiality in the national interest so that it is conventionally less explicit than other heads of expenditure should be. The argument is, of course, both debatable and debated: for example, in the House of Commons and in the United States House of Representatives and Senate.

There isn't much to debate, however, in Tonga. This is how the Defence Vote of the Recurrent Budget for 1990–1 is listed:

Item	Details (sic)	Estimate 1989/90	Estimate 1990/1
9.105	Defence	1,726,000	1,998,360

The rest of the page below is blank, as is the page opposite which is set aside in all other cases for some sort of rudimentary explanation of the whys and the wherefores. As elsewhere, there is no information about the latest annual actual expenditure nor that of preceding years.

Thus, T$2 million unexplained estimated expenditure represents an increase of about fifteen per cent in one year to a figure which critics might in such circumstances uncharitably suspect has been drawn out of a hat.

In no instance of revenue or expenditure estimates is listed the individual accounting officer responsible for its management. The Government pensioners are listed (names and annual pensions) for whatever public purpose that serves.

History, however, is on the side of the Minister of Finance. When in 1890 the umbilical alliance of Tongan Church and State in the person of the Reverend Shirley Waldemar Baker, Wesleyan cleric-cum-Prime Minister, finally came to an end with his deportation, Basil Thomson was sent to underpin the newly appointed Tongan

Prime Minister. One of his first assigned tasks was to ascertain the true state of the finances of the Kingdom. He recorded the initial findings as follows:

> . . . There was, it is true, a Minister of Finance. He was Sunia Mafile'o, the King's nephew. He certainly looked the part of the Treasurer of an insolvent Kingdom. His brow was deeply seamed with the furrows of care, and he spoke little, as befits one upon whose wealth of resources the financial fate of a country hangs. But when the High Commissioner questioned him, the following conversation took place:
> 'What is your office?'
> 'I am Minister of Finance.'
> 'What is the revenue of Tonga?'
> 'I don't know.'
> 'But what is your office?'
> 'Minister of Finance.' (Warmly.)
> 'Well, who knows what is the revenue of Tonga?'
> 'Misa Beika.' (Mr Baker.)
> 'Who takes care of the money?'
> 'I do.'
> 'How much have you got in the Treasury?'
> 'I don't know.'
> 'But you are Minister of Finance?'
> 'Yes; I have told you that I am.'
> 'Well, where's the money?'
> 'In the safe.'
> 'Who knows how much there is?'
> 'Misa Beika.'
> 'Yes; but he's gone. Can't you go and count it?'
> 'No; I haven't got the key.'
> 'Why, who keeps the key of the Treasury?'
> 'Misa Beika.'

It was clear that before the country could emerge from its difficulties some fuller information was required. The liabilities were believed to be very large, and the balance in the Treasury, on being counted, proved to be less than £2,000 . . .

On 17 August 1889, the *Illustrated London News* published the following extract from a recent report by the British Vice Consul in Nuku'alofa:

. . . The only 'public works' carried out last year (no accounts of which are published) were the enlargement of the King's palace, a peal of bells in the King's chapel, a clock in the steeple of the King's church and two houses for the Assembly. The latter, it is curious to note, meets and legislates in secret . . .

In some ways, but apparently not all, it is more than a little different today. Yet I cannot suppress a tinge of nostalgic regret at the disappearance of two posts still on the Palace staff in the 1950s: Keeper of the Palace Records and Palace Clock Keeper.

The salary for the latter was all of £12 per annum. He was not, of course, employed at the Legislative Assembly.

There are other matters of financial management today which are of mounting concern to a not so patient public. One is the business of the quantum of overseas official travel and the allowances paid to those engaged on it. In Tonga it seems always to have been a murky and thus a sensitive issue; albeit one not confined to Tonga.

Twenty years ago in London, a Pacific Island Prime Minister – not from Tonga – and his Indian Ocean counterpart met in scheduled tête-à-tête. Both had come electorally to preside over independent former British colonies.

'Do you travel outside your country very much?' asked the Pacific Island head of government.

'Yes. As much as I can. I am away about half the year for one reason or another. It is the only way I can survive – by supplementing my salary with the travel allowances we have set for ministers.'

It was a hint which the Pacific leader was not to forget. He had already been known to issue instructions for the payment to him of a large lump-sum overseas-travel advance and to refuse to account for it on his return. At least one post-Independence Auditor-General was to give up in despair and resign. The arrogance of non-accountability in the personal use of public funds can become a canker in the body politic. Let it start at the top and its spread will be uncontainable.

Governments broadly use one of two basic systems for the payment of overseas travel costs. The first is the 'actual and reasonable' method. Public funds meet the full cost of hotel accommodation and meals, plus transport and perhaps some entertainment, as paid out by the travelling official from an advance normally given to him before departure. The snag about this method is that its beneficiaries develop an appetite for five-star hotels and fifty-dollar meals, while the key argument is whether 'actual' was also 'reasonable' in the context of Brussels, London, Paris, Washington or Geneva. This lack-lustre practice often runs in tandem with the first-class air-travel syndrome: a matter of status, not cost. It tends to be favoured by some of the poorer and more autocratic Third World countries, where treasurers are ordered to pay up and audit queries go into the wastepaper basket.

The second way, adopted by many governments and agencies, is to use the regularly if belatedly updated subsistence allowances set by the United Nations (per diem is the jargon) for the world's cities and let the official traveller fend for himself. If he goes to an opulent hotel, he will fork out the difference from his own pocket. If he chooses to go slumming or to starve – or gets himself invited out a lot – he will undoubtedly make money and be able to afford his children's school fees and his next BMW. Either way, the standard city rate applies.

Some organisations and governments 'top up' the UN rates in various ways and circumstances, thus encouraging frequent travel 'priorities' and helping to create dependence on a travel allowance income to supplement low basic salaries. Tonga is one of them. The road it has chosen can lead to malpractice and corruption, such as an alleged payment to one minister for a visit to Fiji of T$300 per day when the UN rate was US$96. At the time the Tongan *pa'anga* or dollar was at parity with the Australian dollar at about T$2.50 to the pound.

A minister with some responsibility in these matters went to an Asian country for a week in 1990. I was told that he grossed T$9,000 in that time.

There were many such stories doing the rounds. It is not material whether they were fully accurate or not. The fact that they were in circulation ought to be of serious concern to the ministers who approve the level of payments to themselves and to others closely associated with them. Rectification will only occur if parliament as a body takes a stand. The beneficiaries need to take a long hard look at themselves and what they are perceived to be approving or condoning in their personal interest. The Civil Service too. Some Representatives of the People have set an example by refunding what they regarded as excessive payments made to them. None is remotely wealthy.

The manipulator can, however, go even further. When the costs of an overseas junket are met from UN or other sources of funding, and if the Tongan travelling official claims and is also paid his government's authorised daily stipend, this then becomes straight – or crooked – profit, irrespective of how it comes to be permitted or accepted. There have been murmurings from time to time about double paid airfares, except that it is not the airline which gets the dubious bonus. I remember the decline and fall of an Englishman who was Director of Civil Aviation in East Africa some thirty years ago. It was the practice then, and no doubt still is, for such officers to be invited to be guests of the Farnborough Air Show in England. Permission to attend was granted on this occasion and the cost of his airfare was authorised by said DCA. Fine, except that the airline flew him 'for free' which he thought unnecessary to disclose. The airfare payment found its way into his own pocket and was of use in respect of the expensive divorce proceedings in which he was involved.

'Well,' he said when challenged, 'the Government ought to have had to pay out the airfare. The fact that I got the journey as a guest of the airline was not its business.'

Well, sorry, it *was* rather, argued an outraged Director of Audit when the DCA was charged with defrauding the Government and compromising himself. So a successful professional life was ruined by one piece of corrupt cupidity. He was sacked, pensionless.

I wonder what Tonga would have done in such circumstances.

17

Polynesian Protocol

1988

On 4 July, the King of Tonga was seventy. On the joint anniversaries of his birthday and 1967 Coronation, sumptuous Tongan-style celebrations were planned. Special invitations were prepared in the name of the Government for a variety of distinguished personages in the region and beyond – heads of state, prime ministers, church leaders and others with special Tongan links or relationships; high commissioners and ambassadors accredited to Tonga, plus leaders of industry, communications and non-Government organisations. International aid donors too, of course.

Within Tonga itself a participatory and contributory call went out to nobles, *matapule* and representatives of all districts in Tongatapu, Ha'apai, Vava'u, Niuatoputapu, Niuafo'ou and 'Eua. The seating at the feasts may have been on fine mats, with guests on each side of great *polas* piled high with stone-baked Polynesian food, yet the questions of precedence were no less complex and incident-prone than those in the hallowed halls of high society elsewhere.

But beforehand came the preparation and submission for the King's approval of the invitation list of, to use the word favoured in the Caribbean, dignitaries, from abroad. With royal assent given, the invitations went out and in due course the acceptances began to arrive. One day, in the Ministry of Foreign Affairs in Nuku'alofa, an official took a telephone call from his counterpart in Suva, the capital of Fiji, some four hundred miles to the northwest.

'We have a slight problem which I am sure you can solve for us very simply. It's about the King of Tonga's seventieth birthday celebrations. Our Prime Minister, Ratu Sir Kamisese Mara, has received his invitation and will be very happy to attend. So too will our President, Ratu Sir Penaia Ganilau; but his invitation has not yet been received. His Excellency is sure that it is merely an oversight, and we would be grateful therefore if you would be kind enough to rectify this obviously unintentional oversight.'

He paused. There was no response from the Tongan. So the Fijian pressed on. 'It is, of course, a matter of some slight delicacy. I know you will appreciate how embarrassing it would be for us if our Prime Minister were to be invited to the celebrations marking the birthday of *your* Head of State without *our* Head of State being present. It could mean that our Prime Minister might not be able to come and then Fiji would not be represented at all. I am sure that you would not want that. It would look like a . . .' he coughed gently, '. . . snub, would it not?'

There was a pregnant Melanesian pause to enable the Polynesian to digest all this light-heavy stuff.

'I am sorry about that,' said the Tongan official. 'Let me get my file and check up and then I will get back to you.'

It was indeed a matter of some delicacy as the Tongan well knew; but not quite so slight and not in the way that the Fijian represented it. In 1987, there had been two military coups in Fiji. The newly elected Government was obliterated by force, Parliament was dissolved – unconstitutionally, some contended – and a republic was declared, by courtesy of the gun. Ratu Mara, Prime Minister for seventeen years but beaten in the April 1987 election, accepted appointment as Prime Minister by the new President, who had himself been named and appointed by the coup leader. The twist in the tale was that the first President of this military-created republic was none other than the Queen's representative and former Governor-General, a close kinsman in fact of the man who had overthrown Queen Elizabeth II, Fiji's Head of State. This act of treason, accepted as such by its perpetrator, brought to an abrupt and brutal end 113 years, colonial and post-colonial, of constitutional allegiance to a sovereign in London.

The Tongan royal house, linked by blood, history and geography to the eastern chiefs of Fiji, had mixed feelings, not publicly expressed, about internal military intervention in a country so close, and the overthrow of its elected government. The Tongan has no great love for Fiji's Indians and few are permitted to cross its immigratory threshold. So there was initial, if superficial, empathy with the removal of a so-called 'Indian-dominated government', albeit one led by a western Fijian with Fijian and Indian ministerial colleagues.

But the coups had set alarm bells ringing throughout the South Pacific, and there were signals of further instability to come elsewhere in the area. What would be the effect on Tonga and its hallowed institutions? Do violence to the structure and stability of an adjacent country and what assurance could there be that the Tongan monarchy and its parliament and people would escape unscathed? If not now, then in the future? New Zealand's Maori activists had taken note and said so. Where next then?

Tonga had avoided the question of whether or not to 'recognise' the military appointed 'interim regime' in Fiji by not addressing that question. But the King's seventieth birthday was an occasion of ceremonial Tongan splendour and significance. To be seen publicly to welcome and embrace two Fijian chiefly figures ensconced in the two highest offices of state by the power of the gun gave the royal Tongan sense of conservative propriety a bit of a poser. It was solved initially by the despatch of one invitation – to the Prime Minister, Ratu Mara. Tonga thus adhered to its policy of pragmatism in respect of Fiji's internecine warrings.

So when the Tongan official checked his list, he found that the President of Fiji was not on it. He put the question on paper and submitted it for royal instructions. He pointed out the supposed embarrassment in Fiji and wondered whether the Tonga Government should not now send an official invitation to the President of Fiji as well as the Prime Minister.

The King's response, as it was told to me, said something about how past mingles with present and custom interchanges with proto-col – at will, when there is good reason.

'Since I am deciding who is to come to my birthday party, I included Ratu Mara in the list of guests to whom invitations were to be sent. He is my relation and is also Tui Lau. Ratu Penaia is not my relation. If he is to come, then Kalaniuvalu can invite him, as *his* relation, if he wishes.' So blood was once again conveniently thicker than water and customary chiefly relationships prevailed – or were used to prevail – over public office.

So it was an answer, yet not a decision. The Tongan official thought it prudent not to return that international telephone call. The President of Fiji was not present among invited guests at the royal Tongan festivities. He remained at Government House in Suva. It was there, the rumours said, that the visiting Princess Pilolevu of Tonga had been a guest, a month or so before the first military coup in May 1987, of a less than appropriately decorous heavy-drinking Governor-General, now President of an army-created Republic of Fiji. He has not been to Tonga since.

The perception is that the King had been joking. Whether or not he was at the time, he appears to have changed his mind. On the day before the celebrations began, an invitation to attend *was* sent

His Majesty King Taufa'ahau Tupou IV – a 1990 Silver Jubilee portrait.

Two portraits of Queen Salote: at the age of ten in 1910 *(above)* and *(below)* the last portrait taken in July 1965, some six months before her death.

Right:
The Palace at Nuku'alofa with a carpet of *tapa.*

A shared moment of light relief during the royal visit to Tonga in March, 1970.

Mrs Indira Gandhi, Prime Minister of India, meets the King and Queen of Tonga in 1980.

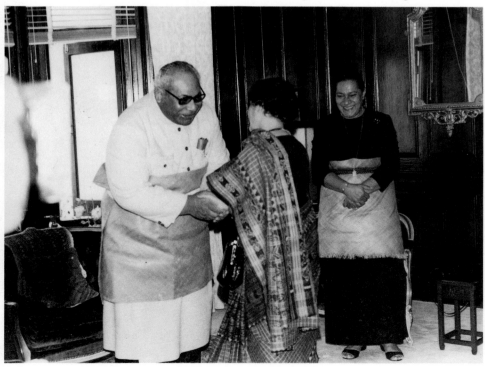

The baptism of the King and Queen of Tonga in the River Jordan, November 1991.

The King inspecting the 1980 Royal Agricultural Show.

Princess Pilolevu in 1987 with her portrait at the age of twenty-one by Australian artist
Mary Edwell-Burke, aged ninety-two. An exhibition of her paintings was held at the
Australian High Commission in Suva, Fiji.

On 10 June 1947, a double royal wedding was held. From the left: Prince Tu'ipelehake, Princess Melenaite, Prince Tungi (now King Taufa'ahau) and Princess Mata'aho, walking on *tapa* cloth to the customary Tongan wedding ceremonies on the day after the church service.

Princess Pilolevu (with Margaret Bain) opening the Walk the World for Schizophrenia charity event in Knole Park, Sevenoaks, Kent, October 1991.

'Elisiva Tauki'onetuku, granddaughter of the former Prime Minister, Prince Tu'ipelehake, performing the solo dance, *tau'olunga,* at a state function.

Into the next generation: Siale Vuki, Melino Lavulo and Anga'aefonu.

His Royal Highness Crown Prince Tupouto'a.

on behalf of the King to the President of Fiji. No reply to it was received.

Relations between the high-ranking houses of Tonga and Fiji in this century have been a mixture of warm kinship and wary circumspection. There are historic reasons. In the eastern Fiji islands of Lau and Lomaiviti, Polynesian physical characteristics and social influences predominate. There are villages today where the descendants of the marauding Tongan adventurers of the past still live; where houses are built in the Tongan and not the Fijian style, and where dress and the first language are Tongan, not Fijian.

In the 1950s, Queen Salote occasionally journeyed to New Zealand where she stayed at the Tonga Government's residence, 'Atalanga, in Auckland. The Queen travelled without fuss or ceremony on the passenger–cargo vessel *Tofua* which made the anti-clockwise 'round trip' from Auckland via Suva, Nuku'alofa, Vava'u, Niue, Pago Pago, Apia, Suva again and so back to Auckland. Because of the ship's ponderous progress round the South Pacific circuit, advice that Queen Salote was on board reached the Government of Fiji well before the vessel arrived.

At Suva, the Queen normally chose to stay on board, where she would receive customary presentations and visits from her Tongan people there – and her Fijian kinsmen. Except for one. The Fijian chiefly leader, Ratu Sir Lala Sukuna, also held the post of Secretary for Fijian Affairs. It was curious that on such occasions, an elusive Sukuna was said to be on horse-back *raikoro* in a remote part of mountainous Viti Levu where he could not be contacted until the ship had sailed from Suva for New Zealand. An elegantly worded message of salutation to Queen Salote and deep regret at his detention on pressingly distant official duty would be delivered to the ship in his absence. The apologia was always emotively persuasive, circumlocutory and couched in courteous but not subservient terms.

The Queen of Tonga would receive the expected communication from Sukuna and inwardly chuckle at the customary gamesmanship of the Fijian high chief. She would accept the message and the personal tributes of the Second XI with composure and decorum. The question was, of course, who customarily outranked whom and who was thus obligated to make the first official call on Fijian soil. There was more than one reason why Queen Salote Tupou of Tonga chose to stay on board her ship while it remained at Fiji's capital port. And, as always, in matters of protocol, Polynesian or otherwise, there is more than one way of skinning a cat.

When the King of Tonga travels abroad today, he usually does so via Samoa or New Zealand. He used to go through Fiji, but has not done so since the 1987 military coups there. So a point is quietly made and delicate questions of protocol are avoided in a land run until recently by a military-appointed so-called interim government.

18

The Man Who Will Be King

He has been represented variously: 'The Honourable Out-of-Step' in the BBC *Radio Times* of 1976; 'Tonga's Cultured Crown Prince' in the *Pacific Islands Monthly* of 1988. However he may be described, one thing is certain: conversation with him is never dull. He sparkles with intellectual vitality. His sentences are littered with penetrating backhanders and unexpected *bons mots*. He is nothing if not disarmingly frank.

'At that disco [in Nuku'alofa], the sound is so loud it doesn't just assault the eardrums. It endangers the rib cage as well.'

'I must say that in my experience old Piggy Muldoon, [the former Prime Minister of New Zealand] was a bit of a shit.'

'What I am most concerned to ensure, as Minister of Foreign Affairs, is the integrity of Tonga: to be trusted as a good citizen of the global village. The currency of your influence in the region is, I suppose, measured by how much your opinion is sought on important issues.'

'I see my grandmother, Queen Salote, as a true Edwardian lady.'

'The old style of customary services has largely disappeared. You've got to pay the going rate now. And never rely on your relatives. They will be the first to steal from you.'

'Of course I have differences with my father. You wouldn't expect otherwise, would you?'

'I suppose I am quite good at palace intrigue.'

'Nothing puts me to sleep quicker than the thought of being King.' (This when HRH was twenty-seven and in London.)

'The royal *kava* ring is a long affair involving sitting cross-legged for hours to see which pigeonhole each member of the nobility fits into.'

Crown Prince Tupouto'a was born on 4 May 1948. Today the mature physique of the Tupou dynasty is apparent. Like Prince Charles, he is having rather a long wait. I suspect that they would empathise with each other.

Tupouto'a is a Sandhurst graduate. He joined the Tonga Foreign Service in 1970; became its Minister Plenipotentiary to the Court of St James in 1975; and has been Minister for Foreign Affairs and Defence since 1979. His interests rival those of Prince Charles: naval affairs and history, tennis, golf, classical music, philosophy, Chinese calligraphy, religious theory and cryptography. At least that is what his personal assistant, Viela, produced for me from her computer when I asked. To her list we can safely add: commercial enterprise and adventurism, and relaxing in the sea, discreetly, on Sundays at Pangaimotu. There, immersed above his shoulders for hours at a time, he holds Neptune-like court. And that is where I found the crown prince when I swam out to present myself on my first Sunday back in Tonga.

Iona, my sister-in-law, lay dying in the mausoleum-like house she had built for herself at Sopu. A year before, she had returned, widowed and divorced, from the wealthy and elegant San Francisco suburbs of Burlingame and San Mateo. Like her mother Matilda in old age, her hair was white, her face unlined. 'Calm of mind, all passion spent', she lay on her bed, cared for by the gentle giant Tita, who had been summoned from Ha'apai by Queen Mata'aho for the purpose.

'The new Tonga: I don't like the way it is going,' she said. 'Money is the central objective now. It's a new way of life, but how can you be happy with five dollars a day for domestic work?'

'How do you see Tupouto'a as King?' I asked.

'He will be terrible. A great mind. A perfect diplomat and raconteur – a joy to listen to. But he can't reach the people. They don't love him.'

I thought about what 'Akau'ola had said about popular perception when Queen Salote died in 1965. The people were nervous, apprehensive, confused then at the prospect of a new King so different in outlook, personality, character and interests. Was it now, a quarter of a century later, to be the same again?

'It is all rather amusing,' Tupouto'a had said to me. 'In the last year of her reign, Queen Salote was the conservative and my father the radical, the innovator. Now he is the conservative and I am thought to be the radical. At nearly forty-three. I always thought that one might be criticised for going too slowly. I was taken aback by criticism that I was moving too fast. Just like sex, I suppose. But a king should be ahead of his people. It has always been so in Tonga. Traditions are not built into concrete. Change is inevitable. I would like to see politico-constitutional change initiated within my father's lifetime. I would then preside over its performance.'

Small countries can be tempted to take themselves too seriously. To others, their problems and preoccupations can seem boringly parochial unless, like Singapore, they display sustained developmental energy which sets them apart from the ordinary. Then, it seems, there is a price to pay in nepotistically controlled government with limited press and speech freedoms; and you run into the question of why one ethnic culture or race can do or achieve what another apparently cannot.

The parish-pump introvertedness of some but not all of the smaller Caribbean islands is the lack-lustre end of the line. They demonstrate a cultureless vacuity and are the more aggressive perhaps as a consequence. In Tonga, this is certainly not so. An historical cultural inheritance and social structure are its distinction and perhaps also its liability: distinction, because its traditions are what have made it what it is; liability, because it is nobody's good news to reflect that there is bound to be massive social change in the twenty-first century. Urbanisation and money will do it, if the politics of the people do not.

I wrote in 1966: 'Contemporary Tonga is a study of custom in transition.' If that was true then, what we have twenty-five years on is a great swirling maelstrom of uncertainty as to what the future holds when the next king takes his seat on the throne. So I asked the Crown Prince what he thought would be the worst scenario for the future of Tonga. He replied without hesitation: 'Entering the new century without a sense of direction.' And, he implied, he would like to provide it. His Royal Highness was in no doubt either about the role of the modern monarch in an all-pervading commercial world.

'I see myself,' he said, 'in the tradition of the merchant princes. Tongans are pragmatists, some might say opportunists. Hence Royal Beer, for example. I am the chairman of a private company but not the majority shareholder as some people seem to think. I looked around to find a reputable national brewery that was not already operating in or shipping to the South Pacific: one of quality, professionalism and financial integrity. The first premise immediately eliminated breweries in Australia, New Zealand, Holland, Denmark, Britain, the United States and France. I hit on Pripps Breweries of Stockholm. They have an impeccable record in Sweden, but are not especially well known outside. It seemed an appealing concept to me that the Scandinavian Kingdom of Sweden should combine, so to speak, in an innovative commercial venture with the Polynesian Kingdom of Tonga.'

I asked about the capital holdings, in respect of which rumours abound.

'The authorised capital is one and a half million Tongan dollars. Pripps has fifty per cent; I have thirty-five per cent. The other local shareholder has fifteen per cent. All fully paid up. My share is from my own money. We produce about a thousand cases per month of five per cent alcohol beer; and only sixteen cases of two per cent light beer. It is all for the local market. The little shops selling Royal Beer in the villages mean that it is not now necessary to come into town to drink. It is done within the constraints of village and family. The end of Tongan society was predicted from the pulpit, but it hasn't happened. In fact the reverse is the case, because crime and alcoholically induced urban brawling have virtually disappeared. It has been a very interesting development to observe.

'Let me tell you something else. When I go to San Francisco, I can tell straight away those Tongans who are in regular jobs, who keep their family links and ties and who are still Tongans even though they have lived for years in the United States. These ones are in San Mateo, Burlingame and so on. Then there are the others across the bridge in Oakland. They are different. They are living with Mexicans and other detribalised Hispanics. They have left the Tongan family and lost its influence. They are the ones who get into crime and go to jail. Tongans are no good outside the extended family system. They seem to disintegrate somehow. So it is this vital sense of identity and pride of belonging that we must strive to take with us into the next century – all Tongans, irrespective of where in the world they live.'

A family in Minneapolis is testimony to the life-style values advocated by the Crown Prince for New Friendly Islanders abroad. Maikeli and Vake Wolfgramm migrated to the United States in 1963. From seven of their sixteen children has come a unique Polynesian rock group success story; and one which is free from smoking, alcohol and drugs. With chart successes in both North America and Britain, The Jets of Minneapolis are modern-day ambassadors of their heritage. The four brothers and three sisters were chosen from sixteen entries from ten countries to perform at the opening of the

Olympic Games in Korea. The mark of their acceptance in the land of their ethnic roots was a special private performance for the King of Tonga and members of the royal family on a first visit in 1989.

So to yet another, and more intimate, perspective: that of a younger brother. The third son of King Taufa'ahau and Queen Mata'aho was born 'Aho'eitu and named after the first Tu'i Tonga who lived a thousand years ago. Today he occupies a modest office in the Vilai military barracks in Nuku'alofa, headquarters of the Tonga Defence Force. It was there, weeks after my conversations with his elder brother, that I called on the man who, post-Dartmouth, was captain of a patrol boat given to Tonga by the Government of Australia. 'Aho'eitu, publicly, is no more. He has been appointed by his father the King to three titles of nobility, with the landed estates and people who go with them. His Royal Highness is now Lavaka 'Ulukalala Ata and generally known by the first name. He is married to Nanasi, daughter of Noble Vaea and Tuputupu.

Lavaka is a popular royal prince. It soon became apparent why this is. He is courteous, polished, smiles readily and warmly. His laughter is infectious. He wears a green khaki working uniform with the two and a half rings of a Lieutenant-Commander. His hair is cut short, military style. He has the large Tupou body frame, trimmed down.

'I foresee ten to fifteen tricky years ahead. There are people who just want to destroy the system without having anything to put in its place. They implant the seed of dissent that leads to violence.'

'Violence?'

'You can never discount the possibility. It may not seem like it, but it is there in Tongan history.'

'What would you do in response to present dissatisfactions?'

'I am all in favour of full democracy. It is the nobles who are the problem. They know how to give orders, but they don't know how to take them. Some of them are ignorant and drink too much. I suppose that I notice it more because I haven't touched alcohol or tobacco since I got married.'

'Is your father very conservative in constitutional and political matters?'

'You could say that. But I think that Tupouto'a will be a reforming king and will introduce widespread changes. The trouble is,' he added with a smile, 'that he drinks and smokes rather more than he should and he has gout.'

103

'Holding three titles and the landed responsibilities that go with them must be onerous. Do you hold *fono*?'

'Yes, but not the old-fashioned kind where the people assemble to be given instructions and then have to carry them out. I consult my people and ask for their views. I encourage them to speak out, so that we can reach agreed decisions – on a proposed tourism development, for example. It is not the old-style *fono*.'

'You could be King in certain circumstances.'

'God forbid. That is the last thing I want. Everyone thinks that being King is easy – just saying yes or no. But it is not like that at all. And it wouldn't suit me.'

So, I thought as I took my leave, any possibility of a fratricidal Palace revolution can now be discounted. Officially.

19

Foreign Affairs – The Tongan Way

There is an apocryphal story of a French diplomat at one of those tedious receptions. Asked by a naïve interlocutor whether he enjoyed foreign affairs, he replied '*Mai oui*. But of course. *Absolument*. They are much less risky and expensive than those at home.'

Which may or may not account for the fact that a number of the established hierarchy of Tonga find frequent overseas journeyings 'in the public interest' so compellingly irresistible. They are not, of course, alone in that.

I may be coming close to *lèse-majesté* if I reveal that nearly forty years ago the Premier, now the Sovereign, found it possible to be away from his seat of office in Nukuʻalofa for, I calculated, precisely half of the three years during which I was responsible to him. 'Off-island', the British Virgin Islanders would describe it, well accustomed as they are to absentee elected ministers of government.

Nowadays Tonga has a splendid all-purpose two-storey building for the Privy Council, Cabinet, the Ministry of Foreign Affairs and that of Defence. Completed in 1988, it is tacked skilfully on to the old Premier's office, a brick building constructed in 1900. The new one is all glass panels; Sydney Opera House-type angles and tiles; wooden interior panelling; expensive air conditioning; and a huge octagonal black glass-topped table. The Privy Council meets there on Friday mornings, presided over by the King who sits in a great leather chair beneath his portrait in the uniform of Commander-in-Chief. On other only slightly less distinguished days, the Cabinet seeks to cope with a fifty-item agenda. In both bodies, the papers are prepared in English; the discussion of them is in Tongan.

A modest plaque is set into a pillar of the portico of the new building. It reads, in Tongan only: '*Fale Fakataha Kapineti ʻA E Puleʻanga ʻO ʻEne ʻAfio.*'

This says something about the conceptual nature of the institutions of Tonga: 'Meeting House of the Cabinet and Government of His Majesty.'

There is not just one Crown Prince these days who has views about modern architecture, so I asked the Tongan one how he would describe the design of his new building.

'Italian insane I would think,' he replied without hesitation. Which seemed as good a point as any to ask Tonga's royal first Minister for Foreign Affairs and Defence about the foreign policy over which he presides.

'I'll give you two versions – the long and the short,' His Royal Highness said. 'The long one will not be much of a variation on the themes I dispense to diplomatic callers, persistent journalists and, well, you. I perceive our foreign policy as one of relaxed observation of the follies of others, like Fiji for example; and association with a variety of countries some of which apparently still yearn for their own monarchies and who, in a spirit of such understandable nostalgia, can be persuaded to invest a portion of their surplus foreign currency in the perpetuation of ours. It is a source of modest gratification on our part and of achievement on theirs, as they see the visible evidence of their distant investments in sports stadiums, a national cultural centre, conference facilities, small industries and general commercial development like wharves and airports.

'Tonga has not joined the UN: there is no need for us to pay for benefits we get anyway. We don't have to finance an expensive office in Manhattan for what would probably be a series of abstentions – if the Tonga delegation were present for voting time. And I wouldn't require them to be.'

In London, Tonga has its only diplomatic mission, but Brussels is beginning to beckon. The registration number of the High Commissioner's Mercedes is 1 TON, which is not perhaps inappropriate when you consider the body weight of some of its ministerial and other visiting passengers. A High Commissioner is hard put to remember all the countries to which he is accredited. It is not surprising. They are: Britain, France, Germany, Russia, Italy, Belgium, the Netherlands, Luxembourg, Switzerland, Denmark, the European Community – and the United States.

I remember an occasion, long since past, when I was about to go off to represent Fiji at a signing session at the Commonwealth Secretariat in Marlborough House in London. I was telephoned by the Tonga High Commission and asked if I could possibly sign on behalf of Tonga as well.

'We can't get there,' they said. 'Can you do it for us?'

'Well thanks,' I replied, 'for the informal conferment of extra-territorial pleni-potentiariness. Do I take it that my signature will be acceptable in Nuku'alofa for purposes of ratification in due course?'

'Yes, yes. Naturally. Cabinet and Parliament know you.'

'That's what I'm afraid of,' I said. 'But all right. I'll do it. For

Tonga. You will send me a written request and authorisation?'

'Do you think it really necessary?'

'Well, yes, I do rather.'

The Tongan demurred. He couldn't put down that he had to pick up the children that afternoon. 'All right,' he said at length. 'I'll think of something.'

So I found my seat behind the name-plate for Fiji at the big table in the chandeliered main conference room at Marlborough House. The signatures document came round in the alphabetical order of countries. I duly did my stuff in the name of Fiji, arose, and went clockwise round the table to the vacant chair behind the name-plate of Tonga. There I signed again, for a second adopted country, and ignored some raised eyebrows from Secretariat officialdom. No one openly queried this little piece of South Pacific camaraderie.

'Shall I continue?' said His Royal Highness. 'If, of course, it is convenient to you?'

'Yes please. Yes. I am sorry. I drifted off.'

'Very well then,' the Crown Prince continued. 'His Majesty has never had urges to address the world from the podium of the United Nations General Assembly. He can do it just as easily to those who seek audience at the Palace in Nuku'alofa. We are quite good, I think, at one-to-one relationships but personally I am not greatly enamoured of night-long conferences, whether in Brussels or Lomé or the Savoy Hotel in London. *Multum in parvo* I suppose you could call it, plus a strong historic feel for what we have and want to retain and how we should develop it.'

Prince Tupouto'a paused and smiled. 'That's the long version. Now here's the short one. The essence of all this is that Tonga doesn't have a foreign policy, I am glad to say. This baffles just about everybody who comes to see me and tries to find out what our policy is on every conceivable subject. And when I say there isn't one, they gulp a bit and maintain a polite silence while they wait to see whether I am joking. But I am not. I don't believe in policies. Historically, policies have got far too many small countries into trouble with bigger ones. I am not going to preside over that sort of thing if I can avoid it. So I – and everyone in this ministry here and abroad – indulge in a kind of active indolence. It is very relaxing in an angry world . . .

'. . . Certainly I travel a lot. I went to the old Soviet Union three times. That is sensibly educational. I think I perceive things that others may not, and travel enables me to move about with a degree of anonymity which is a refreshing change in some invigorating places from the opera-glass inspections under which I labour in Tonga by day and especially by night. So that is about it. All that I have told you is traditionally based and singularly Tongan.'

What is not so singularly Tongan, indeed not Tongan at all, is the Minister's office. It is an eye-catching array of exotic memorabilia and expensive artefacts from many countries. The centre-piece on his glass-topped desk are two computers and a fish bowl. There are no official files.

'All I need is on my computer. We may well be the first computerised Foreign Ministry in the world: Foreign Minister anyway. I'll show you. If I want to see the last ten years' Government revenue and expenditure figures . . .' His fingers rattled across the keyboard. 'There we are. And the annual percentage increases, adjustments for inflation, sectoral analysis, and so on.

'The Treasury bought a knocked-down jerry-built computer a while ago and placed it against an open window. Road dust got into the wiring and then a rain squall soaked it the whole weekend. On Monday morning when they switched it on, it blew up in flames and they lost the whole of the draft Estimates . . . All rather Tongan too, I suppose.'

His Royal Highness paused while my ex-Financial Secretary mind took in the enormity of this technological catastrophe.

'It was all right though. I had taken the precaution of putting everything on my computer as it came to me. So I think that in the end the Minister of Finance was persuaded that the computer costs of the Minister of Foreign Affairs and Defence were justified.' There was a chuckle of royal satisfaction.

Should you have occasion to telephone Tonga's Ministry of Foreign Affairs and Defence and be asked to wait for your internal connection, you will be entertained by tinkling bells. They may be playing an old American cowboy song called 'Home On The Range'. The words go like this:

> Oh give me a home
> Where the buffalo roam
> And the deer and the antelope play
> Where seldom is heard
> A discouraging word
> And the skies are not cloudy all day.
> Home, home on the range . . .

Could it, you might wonder, reflect the escapist yearnings of the Crown Prince-*cum*-Minister for Foreign Affairs and have been personally chosen by him to deliver a subtle message to his world in Tonga? Especially when you also discover that the Government's internal airline, which has international route ambitions, also plays 'Home On The Range' to its calling customers.

20

It Is Hereby Published for General Information . . .

Have you ever noticed notices? I mean really noticed them, not just glanced and passed on. Like two in Sri Lanka. One cancelling a bus stop read:

> Bus Stopping Stopped

The other, outside government offices in the capital Colombo, said:

> Ministry of Parliamentary Affairs and Sports

Same thing, Christine Keeler and Pamella Bordes would no doubt contend.

My own Post Office in Sevenoaks displayed the following counter notice:

> We have recently installed
> a computer system in this
> post office. Please bear
> with us if there is a slight
> delay in service.

Tonga has some of its own. I didn't expect to find a sign outside a wooden Nuku'alofa building offering:

> Discount Air Travel: Apply Inside.

Or this, hitched to a yacht tied up at Faua wharf:

> South Seas Safaris
> Sail Dive Charters
> See the Beautiful Corals
> and Shipwrecks
> Diving Equipment Available
> $20 Per Person
> Every Think Included [sic]

Just what I had been looking for: the ultimate maritime sanatorium for geriatrics.

Notices of prohibition say something about the country in which they appear and the customs or practices they reflect. At the 'Atele Indoor Stadium of Tonga this appears at intervals round the walls:

No Smoking and Chewing Gum
Inside the Stadium

Peanuts are OK then and accordingly their shells litter the place on boxing nights.

In some of the buses of Fiji:

No Spitting Inside the Bus

Outside the bus is presumably acceptable, or uncontrollable.

In the entrance to the staircase leading up to the office of Tonga's Minister of Education was a prohibiting injunction shakily written on cardboard which always seemed to be falling over:

This Entrance Is Reserve
for VIPs Only. Don't Use It.

Under the disapproving eye of the foyer telephone operator I did use it, frequently. But I am not sure what that proves.

I was travelling behind a Nuku'alofa bus one day and read the following in large letters:

Wear a Seatbelt
or
Wear a $75 Fine
Traffic Authority

'Is that the law in Tonga?' I asked 'Alone, unbelievingly. He was one of the Prime Minister's office chauffeurs and knows about such things.

'No,' he said, 'it just came with the bus.'

Like all official drivers, 'Alone is a mine of information and gossip, especially about things he would not be expected to know. So I learned that the Republic of China paid for the indoor stadium where you can chew peanuts but not gum; Japan, for the National Cultural Centre; France, for the Rugby and athletics facilities which the King rides around for exercise; Japan and Germany, for the long sea-wall that protects Nuku'alofa's new and spacious foreshore; Australia, for the airport extension; and Japan, for the new terminal building at Fua'amotu.

'It is good to be neutral,' said 'Alone who seemed to have learned a bit from the Crown Prince.

There are times when there is a price to pay for all this largesse – as Sri Lanka discovered some years ago when its Ministry of Foreign Affairs was told in clear terms by the French Ambassador that the programme of French aid to Sri Lanka would cease forthwith if it were to be, shall we say, unkind to France when it came to voting in the United Nations General Assembly on the resolution deploring the continuance of French nuclear testing on Muroroa Atoll in French Polynesia. It is indeed true that you can buy silence and acquiescence in international affairs, as Tonga and present-day Fiji know well. But there are never, in my experience, any such policy implications related to bilateral Canadian aid. It is the reason why the reputation of Canada stands high among beneficiary countries, not least in the Caribbean.

The ad-man's hype in the Tongan National Centre brochure makes no mention of who paid for it (Japan) but it does manage this sort of thing:

> The emphasis is on people doing things . . . The Centre is a now, happening place. There are minimum barriers between the viewers and the viewed. What is being made you watch being made . . . You will be enthralled and enchanted by the intimacy and immediacy of the Tongan National Centre.

No doubt. It sounded like an invitation to a sex orgy to me and in daylight too. It should really catch on as a tourist attraction once the word gets around; or at least until the churches put a stop to it.

Notices and plaques abound in Nuku'alofa of this and that opened by His Majesty King Taufa'ahau Tupou IV. On the summit of Mt Zion, all fifty feet of it, behind the Palace and overlooking the ageing wooden residence and offices of the British High Commissioner, are the great directional dish transmitters and receivers of Tonga Telecom. A tablet at the entrance below commemorates the opening on 2 July 1987 by His Majesty the King:

The Tongatapu Tropospheric Scatter
Radio Station for Inter-island Communications

I am still not quite sure what all that means but I know what it does. Pick up your telephone in Ha'apai or Nuku'alofa, Vava'u or 'Eua, Niuatoputapu or Niuafo'ou and your signal will come through this internal centre and on to the equivalent international facilities of

Cable and Wireless at Ma'ofanga. In megaseconds, as they say, you can have Saudi Arabia, Ascension Island, Hong Kong or Istanbul.

There is one commonplace technological step that Tonga has so far failed to take. 'That's something I love the place for,' said Millie, a New Zealand Maori working temporarily at Pangaimotu. 'There are still no traffic lights and parking meters. Once I see traffic lights, I know I'm home.'

There are circumstances in which English and Tongan languages combine, although at first sight you might not perceive it. Tongan words consist of alternating consonants and vowels, and always end with a vowel or vowels. So English words for which there is no Tongan equivalent are adopted into Tongan through a process of 'Tonganisation'. Here are some further examples from the legislature: Minister is *Minisita*; Nobles are *Nopele*; Constitution is *Konisitutone*; Law is *Lao*; Premier is *Palemia*.

The Attorney General and Minister of Justice sits behind a grand name-plate which reads: "*Ateni Seniale Mo E Minisita O E Lao*.' Law and Justice appear to be synonymous in the Friendly Islands.

If you obtain a motor vehicle licence in Tonga, it will read as follows: '*Laiseni* [Licence] *Saliote* [Chariot] *Misini* [Machine].' It will be signed by the: '*Ofisa* [Officer] *Laiseni* [Licensing].

Rather good really.

Tongans are, of course, great absorbers, adaptors, even just imitators of selected foreign practices and procedures. Language is but one example. Look at the old photographs during the period up to the early years of the reign of Queen Salote. On many formal or ceremonial occasions, the male members of the Tongan royal family and the nobility took on the outward appearance of Victorian gentry: black ties, stiff butterfly collars, black frock coats – indeed the sober and sombre manifestations of Wesleyanism overlaid on sweating brown skins in hot tropical temperatures. For the women, it was the ankle-length, enveloping Mother Hubbard, hats and even gloves. As H. L. Mencken has said: 'Christian endeavour is notoriously hard on female pulchritude.'

It was all part of 'fakasivilaise', the civilising of the heathen by the early missionaries, and visible confirmation of the adoption of the values – moral, spiritual and vestmental – which demonstrated that the process of Christian change had been accomplished.

Pretentious and showy, yes; the shadow not the substance, yes. But it was seen as an essential part of preserving an independent state and monarchy and the capacity of both to assume equality in negotiating status with predatory colonial powers. And thus be accepted. In that sense, at least, it was eminently successful.

21

A Matter of Linguistics

The voice is soft and precise with a clipped clarity in the articulation of final consonants. Close your eyes and you might be speaking in English with a mid-European Jewish intellectual. Open them, and you perceive an elegantly tailored Tongan woman in red *muu-muu* with matching lipstick and a beguilingly girlish pigtail.

At forty-five, Dr 'Ana Maui Taufe'ulungaki carried lightly her scholarship and doctorate in linguistics. She laughs easily and her eyes sparkle, yet you discover there is a glint of steel. She is unmarried ('I gave up that idea a long time ago') but she has three children, a girl and two boys, adopted in the Tongan way from among her relatives in the chiefly village of Ha'ateiho on Tongatapu.

Her first toe in the waters of the wider educational world was Epsom Girls' Grammar School in Auckland. This was 1964. Thence Auckland University in 1966–8 for a BA in History and English. Three years later she was in Edinburgh doing a Diploma in Applied Linguistics. Six years after that, at Leeds, she completed her Master's in Psychology; and ten years on, in 1988 she emerged from the University of Birmingham with her Doctorate.

'What was your thesis?'

'It has a rather pompous title: Implications of Language Attitudes to Language Planning in a Bilingual Situation.'

'Yes,' I said. 'Maybe it has.'

'I loved Birmingham. Every minute of it. My landlord had a flat next to Simon Rattle and season tickets for the Birmingham Symphony concerts. I went to lots of them.'

'Who are your favourite composers?'

'Oh, Mahler and Tchaikovsky. I am an incurable romantic. I love my emotion served up on a plate, I suppose.'

'In Tonga too?'

'In respect of Tonga and things Tongan, I am very conservative, a total traditionalist. I lament the passing of the Queen Salote era and all she meant to her people. I first met her in a queue of young Tongan girls in Auckland. She told me all my background and ancestry. More than I knew myself. And I was just – well, anybody. It is odd perhaps that in my case, unlike so many others, my periods away from Tonga have reinforced my belief in my own culture and identity.'

She suddenly looked serious. 'That is why I am now so concerned.'

'About what?'

'We are in grave danger of losing our identity as Tongans. We have been too preoccupied with Western values and priorities. Money is all. Many chiefs don't recognise their full responsibilities to their own people any more. Even the language is at risk. There are certain values and ideas that are uniquely Tongan and can only be expressed in the Tongan language. Lose that and what are we? Cultural loss-makers like the Welsh.'

'And the wider condition of the State of Tonga today?'

'The situation is grave.'

'Grave?'

'Grave. Ninety per cent of the people are discontented about the corruption and inefficiency in government and the continuing lack of accountability in the democratic sense.'

'Is there any difference between Nuku'alofa, the capital, and the rest of Tonga in these perceptions?'

'I thought so at one time. But if you look at the last elections in 1990, it was the same groundswell of support for the Representatives of the People all over the country. In fact urban areas are slightly more conservative than the rural ones. It is the middle classes and the bureaucracy as well as the aristocracy who are interested in retaining the *status quo* . . .

'. . . The people are willing to go to war. They will take their spades and hoes and sticks if they are going to be opposed by guns and bullets. The churches are backing them. 'Amanaki Havea, President of the Free Wesleyan Church, and Roman Catholic Bishop Finau are extremely influential.'

That morning there was news of the latest military coup, this time in Thailand. Yet another apparently corrupt and grasping government had gone to the wall. That wasn't the reason for Fiji in 1987, but it is a frequent explanation.

'I wish someone could persuade the King to understand that it is not just his kingship which is at risk, but the very entity and identity of Tonga and its people: the soul of a nation. Perhaps an outsider can persuade him. None of us appears to be able to.'

She paused. 'Don't look at me,' I said. 'I've been through that before. With Fiji. It doesn't do to be found to be right when you are offering advice from the wings. Your advice becomes less and less welcome and you become sidelined rather than listened to. I wonder why that is?'

'You don't, really. You *know*. And so do we.'

'Tell me,' I said, 'you are saying some profoundly disturbing things.'

'Yes.'

'And you are the Deputy Director of Education.'

'Yes.'

'Are you not perhaps . . . ?'

She interrupted me abruptly. 'No. It is not material. The questions facing us are too important.'

'Can I then attribute to you what you have said?'

'Yes. Anything.'

'Is that wise?'

'Being wise is not what is important. It is doing what one has to.'

'Thank you. One last question. What is the meaning of your name?'

'It was given to my ancestor by the Tu'i Tonga at Mu'a. It means "Fighting with your face turned in both directions".'

22

Legendary Interlude: The Trout, Without Schubert

A long time ago, a man called Nafa lived with his wife, Nifi, in Samoa.

A great Tahitian chestnut tree grew on their land. Nafa and Nifi often noticed that a white seabird flew back and forth above this tree, as if it were searching for fish and they wondered why this was.

One day, Nafa climbed up the tree and there on the top of the trunk he found a hollow with water in it and little fish swimming in the water. He climbed down again and cut a banana leaf. He softened the stalk of the leaf over a fire and bent it into the form of a big cup. Then, carrying the leaf, he went up the tree again. He scooped the fish and the water and the mud into the leaf–cup and brought it all down to the ground.

Nafa and his wife cared for the fish, but the only food they would eat was the sediment in the water.

As the days went by, Nafa and Nifi noticed that the fish were growing bigger and bigger. Soon, they could see, the banana-leaf cup would be too small. They set out from Samoa to look for an island with a freshwater lake into which they could put the fish. They sailed south towards Tonga. They called at Niua and Vava'u, but neither pleased them. Then they came to Ha'apai and discovered the island of Nomuka. There they put the fish in the lake, believing that this was the place that would really suit them. And at Nomuka, the fish grew still more and multiplied. They were what we know as trout.

Nafa and Nifi also remained at Nomuka; and before long the woman gave birth to a baby boy, whom they named Nomu. Some time after that, she had another baby, a girl, whom they named Iki.

Now there was a powerful god named Tafakula who lived at the nearby islands of Kao and Tofua, and this god commanded another god, Ha'elefeke by name, to go and live at Nomuka, so that Nifi and Nafa and their children might have him as their god; and so that he might protect them and their fish.

One day, Tafakula sent an urgent message to Ha'elefeke. 'Take

care,' he said, 'for a god living at the Fiji island of Batiki is planning
to come and steal some of the trout from the lake of Nomuka.'

When he heard this, Ha'elefeke kept guard over the fish through-
out the day and night. Then, after two days, the Fijian god did come.
He waited in his canoe near Kao and Tofua for the darkness to fall.
When Tafakula saw him he sent another message to Ha'elefeke.
'Keep a closer watch than ever,' he said. 'I am sure that he will try
to steal the fish tonight.'

Shortly after dark the Fijian god drew near to Nomukeiki, another
island not far from Nomuka which was named after Nomu and Iki.
Thinking that no one was there, he was startled to hear Ha'elefeke's
voice as he stepped ashore.

'Good evening, friend,' said Ha'elefeke. 'It is kind of you to do
me the honour of coming all this way to see me.'

At once the Fijian god realised that Ha'elefeke had perceived
the reason for his visit, and that he must ingratiate himself with the
Tongan god if his mission were to succeed. So he spoke of the
wisdom and compassion of Ha'elefeke which was well known even
in Fiji, and sought his protection.

'I am afraid of Tafakula, the god of Tofua,' he lied. 'But please be
kind and protect me. Pray let me stay with you tonight and I shall
do whatever work you require of me.'

Ha'elefeke was flattered and took pity on the Fijian god, who had
come such a long way. 'Very well,' he said, 'you may remain here
until tomorrow night. And I may give you some fish for your journey. But I too am afraid of Tafakula, for he is my master; and if you
leave with the fish by daylight, Tafakula will take them from you
by force as you go past Tofua Island.'

The Fijian god was overjoyed at his good fortune.

Next day, they worked in the garden from morning to night.
Then Ha'elefeke went off to Nomuka with a big taro leaf, into which
he scooped some of the mud and water and fish. He brought this
back with him to Nomukeiki and gave it to the Fijian god.

'Come,' he said, 'sail away now while it is still dark, so that
Tafakula may not see you. And when you reach the island of Batiki,
go into the centre of the main village, and throw the leaf down hard.
When you do that, a lake will form there in which your fish will
live.'

And with that they parted.

By the time daylight came, the Fijian god had reached a spot called
Mavana on Batiki; and there he went ashore, carefully carrying the
leaf in the palm of his hands for fear lest it might spill. As he walked

quickly along the path at Mavana, the village chief caught sight of him and asked what was in the leaf. The god with the fish made no reply. Holding tight to his precious parcel he began to run.

Angered by such unaccustomed rudeness even from a god, the chief picked up a stone and threw it straight at the parcel. It burst open – and mud, trout and water fell everywhere.

So Ha'elefeke's instructions were not carried out; but where the fish fell, a little stream came from the earth, the stream that now flows into the sea behind the main village at Batiki. And even today, the trout which first came from the chestnut tree in Samoa and the lake in Tonga can be found there and nowhere else in those islands of Fiji.

And that too is how ideas cross oceans and continents and are planted in unexpected ways in unexpected places: to grow and flourish and nurture the intellectual soil and water which gave them refuge and life. For they are the seeds of scholarship, understanding and culture and the behavioural patterns which mould and shape our lives and minds in an ever-changing kaleidoscope.

23

The Swampus of 'Atenisi

'He is the biggest hoax in the educational history of Tonga: a drop-out from Sydney University. The whole place is a disgrace. It only takes students who cannot get into other schools. It ought to have been closed down by the Government years ago. That it has not is sheer negligence in my opinion.'

That is one view I was given of Futa Helu, the self-styled professor who has presided over his 'Atenisi Institute since 1963 and what he describes as the university division since 1975.

There is another view. 'He is the nearest we have to a Tongan guru. He has done more than anyone else to free Tongan thinking from the strait-jacket of custom and traditional fealty. You must expect some eccentricity from such a person and he does not disappoint.'

Indeed he does not, no more than his spiritual kinsman at the University of the South Pacific, 'Epeli Hau'ofa. Except that Futa Helu is less deliberately provocative.

I don't quite know what I expected when I went to 'Atenisi Institute in March 1991. Yet one thing is certain: it was not what I saw and later discovered.

First visual impressions are ones of dire disbelief. A heterogeneous array of disintegrating wooden structures built on concrete piles is scattered precariously around a watery waste amid a coconut plantation – well, among a lot of coconut trees bending in all directions. The access road into the compound is heavily pot-holed and unfinished like the other semi-arterial causeways which support a motor car under protest. Once in, you reverse out, keeping a close eye on the waters on either side. When the seasonal rains fall, it could become the world's first water-borne educational institution.

We stop shakily outside 'the office' and a cheerful American voice behind piles of papers says: 'I am the Assistant Dean. Can I help you?'

'Yes please. Where can I find Futa Helu?'

'At his house. Over there.' He points across the lake. 'He is seeing some Australian volunteers, I think.'

We make a slow circuit through the waters and arrive at the heart and inspiration of 'Atenisi. Unexpected though I am, I am received with old-world courtesy. Could I possibly come back at three p.m.? I can and do, in sheets of rain. The campus is now worse than Lord's cricket ground on the Saturday of a test match. Huge pigs thrust joyously into liquid mud. A sow feeds her litter on the floor of an empty garage.

I go up some wooden steps into a modest reception room. Family photographs at crazy angles adorn the walls. There is an upright piano and hanging macramé. A cat leaps at insects. Futa Helu wears an open shirt and ankle-length *vala*. His greying hair is combed out, senior common-room style. His feet are bare, his voice soft and deliberate. His way with English words is one of meticulous care and respect. I am served tea and cake by his wife, a gracious solo dancer of the past. An eye-catching daughter, on the threshold of womanhood, slips by in check shirt and jeans. I am told that she is sixteen. Not for the first time, I am conscious of my age. There is a general air of relaxed calm which I find infectious. Already I am feeling at home. I remove my shoes; they seem redundant.

'It all started in 1963 as a small night school, mainly for civil servants. There were not enough places in secondary schools so we opened as a high school the following year. In 1975 we began the tertiary part called 'Atenisi University and a technical workshop. It is all very small: four hundred in the high school and five hundred altogether. We started with associate degrees, but our bachelors degrees are now accepted for post-graduate purposes in Australia and New Zealand. We are opening a masters-level degree course this year. We have a proper graduation ceremony, outside, and the King has often come to present the degree certificates.'

'What does the name 'Atenisi mean?'

'Oh.' He smiled. 'That's the Tonganisation of Athens.'

I groaned. I had missed the point yet again.

'This is a free-thinking place with the classical kind of educational philosophy that was traditional in Europe a century or so ago. We teach Latin and Greek. We try to draw on the lessons of the past and so be able to give warnings of the future.'

'What has been the greatest influence in your life?'

'The Greeks undoubtedly. In the 1950s I studied Greek philosophy as an undergraduate at Sydney University. My Scottish teachers were atheists and theists and gradually I became dissatisfied with education in Tonga. In an old-fashioned way, we may have divorced *doing* from *thinking* here. We are not really interested in the practical effects of our work. Our whole philosophy of education is fundamentally different from that of the University of the South Pacific, for example.'

He looked at me. I had been on the USP Council in its early formative years of the 1960s. So I asked: 'Where funding regional governments, not least Fiji, expect the university to set courses and churn out graduates in accordance with their own perceived manpower planning requirements?'

'Precisely.'

'How is 'Atenisi funded?'

'We are completely independent of Church and State. It is always difficult to make ends meet. We are given a low priority by the Tonga Government. So we have to charge relatively high fees, but we have a growing number of loyal families. We have had to fight to keep our heads above water, in more ways than one as you can see. The land is below sea level here. It's a sort of "Little Venice" that has been called a swampus not a campus. Perhaps there is something symbolic in that.'

'So you seek enlightenment and truth for their own sake?'

'Not entirely. We do not live in isolation from the real world. We have clear perceptions about our own land and continually discuss where it may be heading.'

'And where, in your view, is that?'

'There are important historical considerations. The lower classes have over the centuries been subjected to a prolonged feudal conditioning. They have accepted submissiveness without question, until now. They are slowly being weaned away from their time-honoured wretchedness. Tongans who go overseas come back new people; there are some on the staff here. So we at 'Atenisi are in the forefront of a critical approach to education and society.'

Futa Helu was fifty-six at the time I spoke with him. There are six children aged from twenty to seven. He was obviously a late developer, but now very much a family man and father figure. Tongan respect for those who are older is clearly apparent.

He looks up to the ceiling. 'Tonga is emerging from the medieval period. We are in the birth pangs of change. What happened before the Renaissance is occurring in a small way here. There is a weakening of the traditional aristocracies and a perceptible divorce between Church and State. Free Wesleyan and Roman Catholic Church leaders are working closely together for the first time in our history for humanitarian reasons. Their influence is important in the emergence of a new middle class. They have a common enemy of course: the moneyed Mormon Church. The Mormons have a massive conference in Tonga in July 1991. I am told on the side that the hidden agenda is to "buy up" Tonga.'

'But land in Tonga has traditionally and constitutionally been non-negotiable and non-barterable,' I said.

'It isn't so any more. Money has usurped land as the top objective of the ordinary people. They see what it can do and has done for the aristocracy and those who supposedly manage it in government. A docile non-questioning peasantry is no more, not least because of the commercialism of the King. It is all very Greek really.'

'Are you a Marxist?'

'No.'

'Are you then a monarchist or what I might call an egalitarian?'

'I think of myself as a petty liberal.'

'An *éminence grise*, maybe?'

'It has been suggested, but it is not for me to say.'

'So what of the future – of Tonga, that is?'

The response was unhesitating. 'There was unity in Tonga in the days of Queen Salote. Her memory is kept alive in poetry and song. That is all. Today there is potential for a real and continuing opposition. I foresee a much weakened monarchy without the Free Wesleyan Church as its power base. There is a rift between State, Church and monarchy. The King is not accepted as the titular head of the Church, and the President is no longer appointed by the King as the Royal Chaplain.'

'And the prospect of political or electoral change in the lifetime of the King?'

'Very little. I think that the King will sink into deeper and deeper conservatism. We are beginning to see simmering discontent among ordinary Tongans, as the 1990 elections of Representatives of the People indicated. Violence is perfectly possible. The King has been preparing for that possibility for a long time. The wall and steel fence round the Palace is not just there to keep the pigs and chickens inside. The Tonga Defence Force has by far the largest – undisclosed – departmental budget. The officers are all from the *hou'eiki*; the rank and file from the commoners. It remains to be seen how they would stand up to a popular uprising, if one should occur. I expect to see sweeping changes when Tupouto'a becomes King. I hope that it is not too late.'

Futa Helu paused, then smiled. 'HRH wanted to put me up as a member of the Nuku'alofa Club. I declined. It is not my scene really.'

He rose from his armchair. 'You will excuse me now. I have a lecture to give at four.'

The Professor of Philosophy and Tongan Culture came down the steps and walked, barefoot and in *vala*, to a lecture room. Groups of students on the strips of dry land clutched books and talked animatedly. There was not a *ta'ovala* to be seen.

Power and water were off at the Friendly Islander when I arrived back. Electricity Board employees were up three adjacent lamp-posts making repairs. It took four hours on a Sunday evening.

Such things apparently do change in Tonga. In 1955, the expatriate manager and Tongan staff of the Nuku'alofa Electric Power Board were working frantically all through the night to keep going their last working power generator – for the hospital, the Palace, the deep freezers, and so on. At two a.m. on a Sunday morning, they were arrested by the Minister of Police in person for a breach of the Sunday observance law and taken into custody.

I know. I was chairman of the Board. They rang me from the police station at two-thirty a.m. that Sunday morning.

24

Go North, Young Man

'Well, no,' said Finau 'Ulukalala at Lifuka in Ha'apai to Captain James Cook in 1777. For it was there that Cook and his crew were received by Finau with an outward show of hospitality and warmth: hence Cook named the Tongan group 'The Friendly Islands'. He asked Finau what lay to the north. 'To the north is Vava'u, but I should not advise you to go there,' Finau replied. 'Ships have no safe anchorage and landing is difficult. The people are far from friendly.'

'Probably the biggest lie in Polynesian history,' said the present King when I asked him about it in 1955. Finau was high chief of Vava'u, unsuccessful plotter of Cook's murder and notorious ancestor of the ambivalent Minister of Police in my time. (The title of 'Ulukalala and the lands that go with it are now held by the third royal son.)

So Cook gave up all thought of sailing north to Vava'u, not knowing that he had been hoodwinked into missing the safest and most sublimely spectacular harbour in the South Pacific. So it was not until 1781 that the first footsteps of a *kai papalangi* were placed on the soil of any of the most northerly group of Tongan islands. A Spanish frigate *La Princesa*, under the command of Francisco Antonio Maurelle, stumbled upon Vava'u en route for Mexico from the Philippines. He called the land-locked channel of his anchorage Puerto del Refugio – Port of Refuge – reflecting the safety and security he found during his two-week stay.

I first journeyed north to Vava'u from Tongatapu in 1954. By sea, of course, on the Government wooden ketch *Hifofua* whose wayward habits in even sedate sheltered waters made the voyage a nauseous nightmare, without taking into account the well-fed cockroaches and the hundred-plus vomiting deck passengers. This time it was to be mercifully different. *Inshallah*, as the Arabs say: 'If God wills.' The twice-daily De Havilland Twin Otter service of the Government's own airline, Friendly Islands Airways, makes the journey in seventy-five minutes, against twelve to fourteen hours, and is well worth it.

But alas the Friendly Islands Airways are no more. All Tonga's airline services are now Royal Tongan. I learned this by chance standing in August 1992 on Sevenoaks railway station. There to my surprise I came upon the first modest sales office of Solomon Airlines to open in the United Kingdom. Twice a week a new Boeing 737-400 flies from Auckland to Tongatapu to Vava'u bearing on its white fuselage not only the livery of Solomon Airlines but beneath the windows, in red, ROYAL TONGAN. On 1 July 1991 the two countries of Melanesia and Polynesia became operating partners.

The old terminal building at Fua'amotu was silent and largely deserted at seven-thirty in the morning. Likewise the men's lavatories, but for a different reason:

Urinal Out of Order
Management Regrets Inconvenience

We put down mid-journey at the grandly named Salote Pilolevu Airport of Ha'apai – the central group of islands. The windsock was limp and still. A stationary van with a solitary slim red cylinder constituted the fire tender. The cylinder was designed to throw a dry foam blanket over burning passengers. So I was told.

Half an hour later we were over the glorious eccentricities and convolutions of Vava'u harbour; then down, skimming the coconut trees to Tonga's second 'international' airport (external flights go north to Samoa only). I was met by Masina Tu'i'onetoa, Assistant Secretary in the Governor's office and wife of the manager of Burns Philp's Neiafu store. She had under her command an XOS Toyota Range-Rover-*cum*-personnel carrier in which the King travels when he comes to Vava'u. I was careful not to sit in the royal seat. So through sleepy villages to a sleepy town, not noticeably different from what I remembered, even to the challenging array of pot-holes in the roads.

The old wooden cinema perched precariously on the hillside overlooking the harbour was still there, locked and shuttered. The same faded sign of 1950 proclaims the Fungalelea Theatre but it apparently plays to audiences only about once a week now. The soundtrack is still interpreted into Tongan, by the simple device of a shady masculine figure who stands beside the screen throughout the performance and shouts down the film dialogue. Just as in 1954, the belted-out pre-screening music must be audible in Samoa. But it is all a shadow of the past. As elsewhere, domestic video has taken over.

'What time do you get to bed?' I had asked 'Alone, as he emerged from a video shop clutching four or five packages.

'About two or three in the morning,' he replied. 'If I take four for one night I get them at a cheap price. I have to see them all through at one sitting, otherwise I am not getting my money's worth.' Capital punishment, so to speak.

Vava'u is about to have $12.5 million of EEC money spent on it over the next five years: upgrading the airstrip, electricity extensions, roads and ports improvement. With HRH Prince Tupouto'a as the chairman of the development committee, Vava'u won't know itself in the next decade.

I called on the Acting Governor, the Hon. Tu'i'afitu.

'Are the people of Vava'u still the snobs of the South Pacific — ebullient, extrovert and fiercely independent of Nuku'alofa and all things south?'

'Yes, I think so. The character of the people has not changed, even with improved communications and so on.'

I remembered the term *faka Vava'u* – in the manner of the people of Vava'u – proverbial for what is proud or even boastful in the eyes of other Tongans.

One of the reasons I had come to Vava'u was to see Pat Matheson.

At seventy-eight she was the American widow of a Scottish doctor who towards half a century ago came to take charge of the Vava'u hospital. She writes as Patricia Ledyard and her books tell much about her life at 'Utulei where she has lived for nearly all her widow-hood, alone on that chosen point across from Neiafu without a telephone but with her vast library, the *Guardian Weekly*, the *National Geographic* magazine and at weekends her special Tongan friend Tu'ifua.

Masina organised a boat for me to visit Pat. We had not met for thirty-seven years. She is as trim and as sardonically observant of all things Tongan as ever. Her comments are brief and pithy. She embraces two cultures and two languages, and can still see clearly what unites and what divides, what of one is comprehensible to the other and what is not.

'Tongans understand work in groups, but not individual effort and what it means. Tu'ifua, whose opinions I value on everything, said to me one day about my sealing myself off in order to write: "How wonderful it must be to get paid without having to do any work."'

Masina's boat, with me on board, set off in the opposite direction to 'Utulei. It had an outboard engine and a can of petrol to feed it. The can was nearly empty. We put into a fuelling point five hundred yards up-harbour. The steersman-owner-captain-navigator-engineer leapt ashore, with the can but without speaking a word and without attempting to secure the boat to a nearby bollard. There was no rope anyway. Left to its own devices, the boat showed signs of independent action by drifting away from the landing. I reached out to the jetty deck and clung on, my body gradually lengthening, it seemed, as the boat gained on me. Then it stopped, with a gap of two feet between boat and jetty. My body bridged the gap.

Five minutes of agony later, the fuel-carrier returned with his can, jumped back on board, connected the can to the feed pipe, started the engine and set off in a wide arc to 'Utulei. He still said nothing. For the first time I understood the true meaning of the Tongan motto: God and Tonga are mine inheritance.

Pat Matheson is right, I thought later. Tongans do not understand individual effort and what it means – at sixty-seven. Or for that matter, it seemed reasonable to add, doing work without getting paid.

But Pat Matheson also held the key to a Tongan mystery which I first learnt of a year before in the Caribbean. She was the guardian of documents which I was anxious to see. When I asked her about them, she gestured towards the disorder of her library, with its piles of limp journals, books and papers. It looked as if I had made a global journey to Vava'u, eighteen thousand miles, from the Caribbean, Britain, New Zealand and Nuku'alofa – for nothing. 'They're somewhere in there,' she said, 'but I can't seem to lay my hands on them.'

The rain was sizzling down. I walked through the streaming streets in and out of those now invisible pot-holes. Leopate Taxis, across the road from the theatre, were immobilised in mud. Good, I thought, I got that one – the Tonganisation of 'leopard'.

I passed the Roman Catholic Chanel College where a miniature game of seven-a-side Rugby was in progress – by two teams of piglets surging at speed up and down and across the field all at once.

'I've seen more pigs in Neiafu than the whole of Tongatapu,' I said to Masina who is a 'foreigner' from Nuku'alofa.

'Maybe,' she sniffed, 'it's because the Vava'u people don't keep them inside fences.'

We went, *lento ma non gracioso*, to see a causeway being funded by the EEC.

'They had to get workmen from Tongatapu. The Vava'u people just come each day and sit down and talk and make 'umu and don't do anything. Very strange, those people.' Maybe they didn't want the causeway, I thought rather uncharitably.

There are two admirable new buildings in Neiafu. One is a beauty:

the Bank of Tonga, designed as two round-ended Tongan *fale* with tasteful modern tilings from New Zealand and a glass-studded concourse centre-piece above entry steps. The other is the imaginatively decorated and well-run Paradise Hotel with its splendid panorama of Vava'u harbour. The general perception is that it is superior to Nuku'alofa's International Dateline Hotel. Its restaurant certainly boasts the most sumptuous pizzas that I have ever tasted.

I stayed across the road at the Vava'u Guest House, a modest hostelry owned by Mikio Filitonga, an engaging Japanese–Tongan whose new Swedish managers were undertaking improvements. It was timely, before the start of the new season; but you couldn't really complain, at £6 per day, about having to move the bed around four times during the night to avoid the steady drips from the relentless rain. The food was acceptable and the atmosphere family-friendly. For entertainment, there were the dogs and the cats and the chickens and the lizards and the mosquitoes, plus the erratic electricity supply and the great pigs whose nocturnal adventuring and adenoidal grunting and belching seemed to silence even the roosters. But I missed the toads of Fiji. They would have had a field day – or night.

As export bananas and copra are no more, we went to see the vanilla production on the Government Experimental Farm, and the Small Industries Centre funded by the seemingly ubiquitous EEC and opened by His Majesty the King in 1990. It is regarded as a great success, except that no small-scale industries were housed in it.

There was some ferociously frantic club Rugby on a muddy shower-swept pitch below the King's Vava'u palace. I thought the refereeing hard to follow and the play noisy and scrappy, even before sustained rain came back and put paid to anything approaching co-ordinated teamwork.

Two Japanese girls liked it. 'Exciting,' they said. 'Just like Jahpahnese Rugby. English people,' they announced, 'like tea and classical music. We like Mozart and Stravinsky.'

The second night was worse than the first. The wind howled and raindrops pelted through the roof, ceiling and the mosquito-wire netting in the windows. I put all my papers and writing materials under the mattress of the second bed. If you come to Vava'u in March, bring three umbrellas. And don't attempt to write.

On Sunday morning it was not noticeably any better. Masina drove me to the Wesleyan church through pot-holes which were becoming positively cavernous. As the service was about to start, the skies opened and the rain and wind returned with a sustained ferocity that rivalled the fervour and all but drowned the opening singing, which I would not have thought possible.

The young man who conducted the choir and the general singing looked familiar. Yes, he was the swaying bass guitarist in the Paradise Hotel show band the night before and the official driver who had taken me in PM17 to call on the Governor on the morning of my arrival two days earlier. Maybe he is a Vava'u Rugby player in disguise as well.

The choir sang 'The Lost Chord' and, with the congregation, 'Joy to the World', in Tongan of course. The last time I had heard it was in the Kid Ory jazz band version broadcast from the United States Virgin Islands. Christmas 1982.

As older Tongan ministers will do, the *faifekau* put out his pulpit message at full volume, rising in the peroration to the high-pitch level of incomprehensibility of a horse-racing radio commentator. The closing benediction was delivered by a member of the congregation who was not disposed to relinquish lightly his moment of glory: he took all of seven minutes. We returned to an embattled Vava'u Guest House. My afternoon harbour sail had to be cancelled. The weather forecast still said 'occasional showers'. The wise heads sniffed the air for early signs of a hurricane. I began to have doubts about my passage on the German-built ferry *Olovaha* which was due to sail from Vava'u to Nuku'alofa via Lifuka and Ha'afeva in the Ha'apai group at seven a.m. next morning. It no longer seemed such a pleasant prospect. Somewhat belatedly, the forecast, which comes from Nadi in Fiji, said something about storm force winds and rain in Vava'u. As if we did not know.

The *Olovaha* departure was delayed until ten p.m. on Monday. Doubts returned about the wisdom of my maritime expedition south, and when it would begin and end. Or if. After all, the ticket said quite clearly: 'Only valid for the voyage as started (sic) on this ticket.' That night there was a ferociously red and angry sunset.

'It's all over,' said 'Afeaki, at the Paradise Hotel. 'It will be a lovely sunny day tomorrow. The depression has moved away to the east.' He is a People's Representative and goes out fishing and should know about these things, I thought.

But no it hadn't – or didn't – move away east. On Monday morning, it came back again with low murky cloud, gusting winds and that familiar driving rain. I thought it time to cut and run.

'Can you get me on the afternoon flight to Nuku'alofa?' I asked a patient and helpful Masina.

'Yes. If it comes,' she said.

We drove through the slush and mud and rain to Vava'u International Airport. It too was awash, the check-in staff sheltering behind an *ad hoc* cardboard contraption on the counter. The weighing-in equipment, like the Minister of Finance, had history on its side. It was one of those heavy Victorian period pieces with iron weights which moved along a horizontal scale and gave measures that were wild approximations.

After half an hour, the fire van set off out into the mud and contrived to back up a small grassy mound. 'In case it can't start, it can run down,' said Masina, speaking apparently from experience.

The Twin Otter, appropriately named, emerged through a swirling cloud base – at about a hundred feet it seemed to me – and put down in a stream of spray and mud. At last I had before me a Tongan 'flying canoe'.

'That's the agent for the *Olovaha*,' said Masina pointing to a disappearing female form of sizeable proportions. 'The ship is postponed again for twenty-four hours until ten p.m. on Tuesday night.'

We landed in something like sunshine at Fua'amotu. All was calm and peaceful. The Friendly Islander lived up to its name. It was another world. 'A home away from home,' said Papiloa, whose place it is. 'What would you like for dinner?'

I asked for fresh fish, grilled. 'Ila went out for some. Then she washed and cleaned them in the sea as I swam nearby. Not a shark in sight. The fish and rice were ready at seven-fifteen as she had promised. When I had finished, I said: "Ila, I just feel like some of that ice-cream you bought specially for me before I went to Vava'u.'

She looked askance. 'I got red eye, Bain. The sickness come to me. I off now.'

'And the ice-cream?'

'Sorry, Bain. *'Aisi kilimi osi.* It's finish.'

'But you bought it for me and I haven't had any.' I sounded querulous. I suppose I was. Tired too.

'I know, Bain. The staff eat it. They hungry and I forget to lock the refrigerator.'

25

Malaspina's Bottle

'It's all very unfair,' they had said to me. 'When March comes, you would never know how glorious the weather is in Vava'u for the rest of the year. We should shut down in March – like the French and the Swiss – and not let anybody come.'

As events turned out, I am glad they don't.

Nearly a year before, in April 1990, I had sat in the British Virgin Islands talking with Ross Norgrove – not about the Caribbean but about Vava'u and what happened there two hundred years earlier. Ross Norgrove was an old New Zealand coastal mariner who ended that part of his career as master of the Auckland Harbour Board's venerable steam tug *William C. Daldy*. Then he set off for Fiji and Tonga in his *White Squall I* which he chartered until the Caribbean called and he did the same there. He went back to the Pacific for a time and in 1973 was in Vava'u with his splendid seventy-foot schooner *White Squall II*. And it was at this point that Allessandro Malaspina and Pat Matheson came into the story.

In 1793, exactly two hundred years ago and twelve years after the Spanish first discovered Vava'u, came two more Spanish ships, the *Descubierta* (the Discovering) and the *Atrevida* (the Daring), under the command of an Italian, Don Allessandro Malaspina. He had already surveyed in Doubtful Sound and Dusky Bay on the south-west coast of the South Island of New Zealand, being aware of them from the Cook charts.

'It would be difficult,' Malaspina wrote in his account of that investigation, 'to give a more complete and accurate description of the ruggedness and elevation of this coast than that given by Captain Cook on his first voyage.'

Maybe so, but Malaspina's precise narrative of his own venture into Dusky Bay and Doubtful Sound suggests that he would have applied similarly high standards of seamanship and navigational accuracy to his investigation of Vava'u harbour, both of which would prove crucial to our solving a mystery.

Ross Norgrove had told me that Pat had in her possession a photocopy of an old manuscript in Spanish of two centuries before. She

133

showed it to Norgrove's wife Minine, who is from St Croix in the US Virgin Islands, and is bi-lingual in Spanish and English. Even so, it took her three weeks to translate the document, sitting on the deck of *White Squall II*. She then put the results in English on tape. It turned out to be the log of Malaspina's expedition in which he alleged that he had buried a bottle on a tiny Vava'u island with a chart and parchment inside claiming Vava'u for the King of Spain. These were the documents and tape which Pat Matheson could not find for me.

Malaspina had sailed from the east through the Marshall and Caroline Islands to the Philippines. Then he went south-east to the northern coast of Papua New Guinea, thence south of western Fiji, Norfolk Island, the south-west coast of New Zealand and across the Tasman to Port Jackson. From there, he sailed to the Kermedec Islands, then north up the eastern seaboard of Tonga, round the top and back down circling west and away east. After Vava'u, he visited Tongatapu and 'Eua in the course of his departure from Tonga.

The expedition's voyage lasted for five years from 1789 to 1794. The Tonga section is contained in chapter five of Malaspina's account. In the typed version which Pat Matheson has (Segunda Edición, Madrid 1885) there are twenty-eight extra-long, double-column, double-spaced pages. Malaspina was nothing if not meticulous. The complete document (the original Spanish of which may be found in the Appendix) is headed:

Scientific/Political Mission
around the World
aboard the ships
Atrevida and *Describierta*
Under the command of Naval Captains
D. Alejandro Malaspina
and
Don José de Bustamente y Guerra
From 1789 to 1794
Chapter V

The journey from Port Jackson to the Friendly Islands was broken at the Bay of Maurelle in the Archipelago of Vavao where a reconnaissance of the islands was undertaken.

Here is Minine Norgrove's taped translation of what Malaspina wrote on 30 May 1793, dictated as she sat on the deck of the *White Squall II* in June 1973:

The pilot of the vessel Hurtado had orders to bury in the spot where the circularim [the tented observatory set up on the island] was a bottle which enclosed the authentic papers of our arrival and of the possession we had taken of all the archipelago in the name of His Majesty with the consent of Vuna himself; and so that this solemn act would have greater authenticity in the presence of the naturals (natives) and as notice for those who come after us in those seas, now the buried bottle was dedicated with our insignias and flags and then saluted. We saluted these in the presence of both crews with seven times the 'Long Live the King'. Then the naturals called on the *Descubierta* and, in imitation of Vuna, made the same number of acclamations.

The rest of the day was quite pleasant. It was occupied on our part and that of the naturals in allowing our social instincts the freedom to act as we chose . . .

It was a telling picture – Vuna, the chief who held suzerainty over the island, diplomatically exhorting his natives to echo the Spanish huzzahs. I was puzzled by this easy conquest. And there I was in the Caribbean, with the document and tape across the other side of the world.

The news of the manuscript and what it contained was immediately conveyed to King Taufa'ahau, who gave permission to Norgrove and Matheson to set out in search of Malaspina's island. 'There was one royal proviso,' said Norgrove. 'The King told me: "If there is a bottle buried, on any island, with a paper inside claiming part of my territory for another country, then I am going to be the one to find it. If therefore you do identify the island, I don't want anyone to go ashore."'

'So those were the King's instructions,' said Norgrove, 'as we set off on a beautiful calm day to find out where exactly the ships of Malaspina had anchored. What had puzzled me was this: the compass bearings were given true in the old quadrangle notation like, for instance, north to east, then south up to east, then south up to west and north down to west. So this was all right and I could calculate where he anchored latitudinally. The longitude, however, was way out. In those days, the chronometer was only just coming into use, but as this was a well-equipped expedition, it was reasonable to suppose that Malaspina had one for ascertaining longitude. And then I discovered his longitude for Port Jackson (Sydney) was the same number of degrees out – 6° 12' – as the bay in which he had apparently anchored in Vava'u. So then I wondered what he had used as the prime meridian. When I looked up the longitude of Cadiz, I found that he had used Cadiz, not Greenwich, and everything fell into place.'

'You stumbled on the key to where Malaspina had anchored?'

'Yes. A hunch, because it was a Spanish expedition. I was thus able to pinpoint the anchorage at a small island in a deep bay with open sea off the south-west coast of Vava'u and outside the entrance to that glorious tangle of islands through which you thread your way to Neiafu. We set off in *White Squall II*, using only the engine, and at the harbour entrance we turned right and sailed north off the coast to the northernmost point of Vava'u. Then we turned round to sail south as we sought to simulate the passage of Malaspina on his arrival all those years before. With Minine's tape for guidance, the whole picture began to unfold before us. I remember that there were two bearings for the anchorage of the Spanish ships. One was a conspicuous high needle-shaped rock that Malaspina had described; and it *is* conspicuous, just off a point. It was on our port hand coming down as we turned into this deep bay, almost at right angles to what was another bearing ashore. All I did was keep the ship's stern on the bearing of the needle-shaped rock until I got the other bearing lined up so that they crossed.

'And this undoubtedly was the biggest moment of the whole trip: our echo sounder was pinging away on twenty-three fathoms, the precise depth that Malaspina had recorded as his anchorage.'

'So you had reached the point,' I said, 'when modern technology gave you exactly the same depth of water as the lead line had given the Spanish expedition nearly two hundred years before.'

'Absolutely. And from there,' said Norgrove, 'was a compass bearing to the islet – it was no more than about two thousand square feet – separated from the mainland. On that little island Malaspina's scientists set up an observatory in a tent to carry out experiments about gravity and compass variation. Malaspina duly claimed the islet and all its Vava'u neighbours for the King of Spain and put a chart and a record of this in a bottle. Before they left after some weeks, they buried the bottle in a hole below where the tent had been and smoothed over the ground. We positively identified the islet, there is no doubt about that. I checked the compass bearings a dozen times, and the sounding. The water was so deep, we lay off at about thirty feet – a typical Vava'u island, rising sheer from the water to the height of the masthead. But as the King had ordered, we did not go ashore.'

When the results of the Norgrove investigations became known to the King in Nuku'alofa, there was a swift royal response. Some fifty prisoners were despatched north to clear the island, erasing all its trees and undergrowth. At the landing place, they built a flight of wooden steps with a railing. When all was ready, the King came on a landing barge with a retinue of retainers – and Pat Matheson. Then the search began for Malaspina's bottle.

It was to prove elusive.

When in due course the King left, not concealing his disappointment, the prisoners stayed on at their fruitless excavations for over a fortnight.

'Then one day,' says Pat Matheson, 'some of them came to me. They begged me to write on their behalf to the King, pleading that they be allowed to return to Nuku'alofa; the season for the planting of yams was nearing its end, they said. So I wrote to the King who graciously agreed to allow the prisoners to end their labours in Vava'u and go back to their prison gardens at Hu'atolitoli.'

The island thus reverted to peaceful loneliness, holding firm to its solitary secret.

It was the morning of Monday 11 March 1991. The sailing of the *Olovaha* had been delayed again until ten p.m. that night. The rain and wind were unrelenting. At eight-thirty a.m. there was a gentle knock at the door of my *fale*. Pat Matheson stood outside, clutching a parcel enveloped in wet polythene. She had somehow got herself across the harbour from 'Utulei to Neiafu. I pushed wide the door and she came inside.

'I've brought you these,' she said, as she unwrapped the Minine Norgrove tape of 1973 and her copy of the Malaspina manuscript. If the ship had not been delayed by the misbehaviour of the Vava'u weather, I should not have seen them.

'Was there a bottle, do you think?'

Pat Matheson holds many of the secrets of Vava'u. 'Yes, I believe so,' she replied. 'My guess is that Vuna took it.'

Now that seemed more than just a possibility. The Tongan chief might not have been as keen as he seemed on the prospect of Spanish sovereignty over his domains. Maybe another example of Vava'uan trickery had preserved that part of Tonga – for Tonga.

26

Just Call Me Pat

Bishops, like headmistresses, strike a sort of fear in me. In advance. The naughty or sinful boy resurfacing, no doubt, plus an unhealthy spiritual scepticism. So I approached my meeting with the first Tongan to be appointed by the Pope as Roman Catholic Bishop of Tonga with a touch of apprehension.

There was no need. I had asked Loka Mafi to make the arrangements. He it was, in 1955, who created mayhem in the Premier's office one afternoon by suddenly disappearing when he was supposed to be setting up the *Daily News* for issue at four p.m. He had a date at the registry office – to be married, it later transpired. Religious ceremony thereafter, but no honeymoon. In 1991, sobered into more orderly behaviour by over thirty-five years in holy matrimony, Loka headed the philatelic bureau in the Government Treasury. Neither of us recognised each other at first, the respective deteriorations of age being an effective disguise. But Loka's Catholic connections were durable and influential. He duly set up the meeting.

Heat and humidity notwithstanding, I dressed in tie and jacket. Bishop Patelesio Finau received me in an open-neck blue and white Hawaiian-style shirt. The only evidence of clerical office was the cross and chain round his neck. He was holding a copy of my 1967 *The Friendly Islanders*.

'I've always been greatly intrigued by this,' he said, 'from the King's foreword: ". . . So Tonga is always trying to get the best of two worlds – or of all worlds if there are more than two . . ." I have often wondered what he meant.'

I pondered this unexpected opening. 'The spiritual world and the natural world and, maybe, the material or monied world. That could be right for the present anyway.'

'Yes.' The Bishop was reflective. 'But I suppose we shall never know for certain . . . How did the concert end?' By coincidence he and I had met and sat together the previous evening at a charity jazz concert at the 'Atele Indoor Stadium by an Australian jazz band from Melbourne supported by local bands and choirs. Round the other way as it turned out. The Australians did not get to work until eleven-fifteen p.m., three and a quarter hours after the start. Queen Mata'aho, although unwell, nobly stuck it out till midnight; Bishop Finau had wisely slipped away much earlier. So later, in droves, did half the tired and heat-exhausted audience, many of them schoolchildren.

In the Bishop's office next day, we were not therefore meeting for the first time. I too had something in my hand: the latest edition of the Vava'u Press news magazine *Matangi Tonga*, with a splendidly robed Bishop Finau occupying the front cover and a penetrative article within by editor Pesi Fonua. Highlighted on the cover: 'Bishop Finau speaks out against tyranny in the home and state.' 'And who,' said King Henry II of St Thomas Beckett, 'will rid me of this turbulent priest?'

There are two kinds of Church leaders. One speaks out on matters of public interest and concern and gets told not to interfere in the business and responsibilities of government. The other is silent on such matters, concentrates from pulpit or press on spiritual issues and pastoral concerns and gets told that the Church is out of touch with the real world. There is no doubt which kind of Church leader Bishop Patelesio Finau is.

He has held his office since 1972 when he was thirty-seven. He leads by example a dynamic influential minority Church. The mark of his personality and humanitarianism is on it everywhere. 'There are matters of importance today on which I must speak out. So I do so, and have been called a Marxist by the King, and an agent of the Pope by the Crown Prince, with a curious absence of consistent reasoning in both cases. Political policies and actions touch on morality and human rights and the dignity of people as individuals. You can no longer assume automatic acceptance or compliance in Tonga. People have to be convinced today by consultation. The Church is now questioning the structure of our society of which the Government is part. But if you criticise, you are assumed to be seeking to destroy. My criticisms are constructive, but they are not received that way. I spent about four hours one evening with Noble Fusitu'a. He seems to specialise in heated debate. We disagreed on just about everything.'

'You appear to have an interestingly close working relationship with the President of the Free Wesleyan Church, the State Church.'

'Yes, we do. It is something to which I attach special importance – and to our membership of the Tongan Council of Churches. In fact, we are meeting this afternoon to agree the terms of a letter conveying our concern over the recent ill-advised and hasty amendments to the Constitution about the naturalisation and sale of Tongan passports.'

'This is a new Roman Catholicism – working with other Christian Churches.'

'It reflects our shared fidelity in being disciples of the Lord. Our common ground is in gospel values in the world of today.'

'Seeking solutions to basic human problems and needs rather than pursuing theological arguments which divide?'

'Yes. In effect.'

I looked at the story in the newspaper, *Matangi Tonga*:

Our people are coming of age and they should be given power. Our system now with nine Members of Parliament representing 100,000 people, and nine Nobles Representatives representing thirty-three nobles, and twelve MPs appointed by the King is just ridiculous. One day our grandchildren will laugh at how foolish we are. I mean, I just laugh at us now. If our King and nobles were *papalangis*, we would not let this happen; but we have been fooled by the fact that they are Tongans, our own people.

'If the nobles ever had to make a choice between Christ and the King, there is no doubt that for many of them, the King would win. Well, some. Yes, some. Intellectually they still live in the days when the King's *matapule* were entombed with him when he died.'

'Did you ask the King why he called you a Marxist?'

'Yes. I went to see him afterwards and put the question, but I never got an answer. After an hour, I gave up and talked about other things.'

'The problem of power and who exercises it concerns you?'

'Yes. Some of those in power use it unwisely, just to show off that they have the power.' And, I thought, sometimes to show that they believe themselves to be above the law.

'Is there suppression in Tonga?'

'Yes: in the domineering attitudes that prevail right down to the village and even family level.'

'With this sort of ensnared consequence perhaps?'

> *The Cycle*
> When you have suppression
> There will be resentment.
> And when you have resentment
> There will be resistance.
> And when you have resistance
> There will be violence.

And when you have violence
There will be suppression.
And when you have suppression . . .

'Well, I hope not violence – in Tonga,' the Bishop said. 'I am a pacifist. Revolution in the heart, yes. No more.'
I showed him this:

Liberty and property can co-exist.
But if you put property above liberty,
You will lose both.

Maximilien Robespierre
France 1789, the year of the
French Revolution

'Yes. That is precisely what I fear for Tonga.'
'One final question. What is the meaning of your name Patelesio?'
'Oh. It is Patrick. First into Latin, then the usual Tonganisation.'
'Thank you, my Lord, for allowing me to come to see you.'
'A pleasure, Kenneth; and – just call me Pat.'

Another cleric, another generation, another Christian religious persuasion but, perhaps surprisingly, not all that different – in essential non-ecclesiastical matters, at least.

The Reverend 'Amanaki Havea was the President of the Free Wesleyan Church of Tonga. He held the annually elected post from 1971. He was to retire at the age of seventy in 1992. The *Matangi Tonga* story about him is headlined 'One Man's Quest for Church Unity'.

It was Sunday morning. I went again to the main Wesleyan church in Nuku'alofa. Thirty-eight years intervened, but my memory was alive to the riches of the massed choirs singing the Sanctus from the St Matthew Passion on the occasion of the first royal visit of Queen Elizabeth and the Duke of Edinburgh in 1953.

One of the groups chosen on that resplendent December day was the Maopa Choir, the King's own. They were on choral duty again on Sunday 24 February 1991, with their brass band, rich and resonant as the sound soared into the rafters of the great open church. Four rows of women, two of men, and the band behind. But fifty altogether, with the sound of thrice that number. The choir master presided, imperious, on top of three wooden steps: white jacket, white shirt, blue tie, beige *vala*, *ta'ovala* – and below, bare legs and bare feet.

A welcome and text in English: service and hymns in Tongan. I stayed on at the end, to listen to the last post-service *réjouissance* by the choir. By then, the church was all but empty. Overtime – for the exuberance of shared devotion. Not money. And that is how I came to meet 'Amanaki Havea, after that prolonged interval of years.

'You are no longer also the Royal Chaplain?'

'No. I resigned the chaplaincy in 1977 when I went for five years to be principal of the Pacific Theological College in Fiji. There has been a separate appointment since then. It suits everyone, I think. I am free to represent the Church and to assume the prophetic view. It means that I am some distance from the King now, but as chaplain I would not be free.'

'Does the King still come to church?'

'Regularly. But not here. At the new church at Fua'amotu, near the royal residence there.'

'Does the King seek your advice?'

'I don't enjoy the same kind of relationship as in the past. In the main he will seek the chaplain's advice when there is need.'

'You do not regard him as head of the Church any more?'

'He never was the head. He is a member only; but of course, a very important and significant member. Even Queen Salote was very clear and adamant that she was just a member.'

'Your relations with other Churches?'

'Warm and cordial, among members of the Tonga Council of Churches, that is.'

'And with the Roman Catholic Church?'

'Especially productive and frank. This new development is entirely due to the enlightened perspectives of Bishop Finau.'

'How do you see the Church in parliament in Tonga?'

'I don't. Not with seats anyway; but twenty-four of the thirty members of the present Assembly belong to the Free Wesleyan Church.'

'And the future structure of parliamentary representation?'

'I am not a supporter of the notion of an upper and a lower house. That would be unnecessarily expensive and would still divide the nation. I believe that there should continue to be one house, but that its identity should be very different.'

'There seems to me to be a great deal of unease at present. Simmering discontent, perhaps.'

'I agree. In my opinion all our trouble stems from the top. The King is hungry for money. The ministers do their best to protect the Crown. Sometimes I wonder how they manage to continue doing it. The King and the Crown Prince are totally different. The King has grown more and more resistant to change. His interest is only for himself. His associations – money-making – in Australia, Canada, the Philippines and Japan are all of a questionable nature.'

'Do you foresee violence?'

'No, I do not. That is not the Tongan way any more.'

'And the future, after the King dies?'

'I have hope in Tupouto'a. As a man he is real and genuine; and his frustrations are deep. He has grown so long under a thick bush and not been allowed to come up to the sun.'

It was not quite how the Crown Prince had seemed to me, but no matter. There was a fair point to be made. The King had been appointed Premier when he was thirty-one. Tupouto'a is forty-five.

'The Prime Minister, Tu'ipelehake, has been handicapped by ill-health for so long. Day-to-day government has been virtually leaderless. It is very sad and tragic. There has been an obvious solution, but it has not been adopted.' (This was in 1991.)

We shook hands as I got up to go.

'Don't forget the vision,' 'Amanaki Havea said. 'The vision of the future of Tonga.'

'Oh dear. Yours or mine?'

'Yours, of course,' he said.

'I haven't reached that stage yet. And may never do so . . . But I suppose that if you bury your head too long in the sand you are likely to get washed away, sooner or later.'

The Constitution of Tonga empowers the Head of State to appoint all Ministers of the Crown; and in those Friendly Islands of the South Pacific, he or she who appoints does not normally dis-appoint. So it was that Tungi, having become King Taufa'ahau Tupou IV in 1965, then named his younger brother to succeed him as Premier and later Prime Minister. It was a post which Prince Fatafehi Tu'ipelehake, the second son of Queen Salote Tupou III and Prince Viliami Tupoulahi Tungi, was to hold without interruption, and without having to face the polls, for close to twenty-six years. It is easy to see why he was most frequently the longest-serving prime ministerial incumbent at biennial Commonwealth Heads of Government meetings until August 1991 when ill-health compelled his retirement.

The two royal brothers were comparable in size and weight (at least seven hundred pounds between them for many years) but they were widely different in temperament, personality, intellect and style. Tu'ipelehake's more modest scholastic attainments can be attributed to Newington College, a Methodist secondary school in Sydney, to which royal Tongan sons and those of the nobility were often sent; and to Gatton Agricultural College in Queensland. It is true that the younger prince had no pretensions to intellectual stature. Indeed, you could say that he spent all his life – not only in that respect – in the shadow of his elder brother, the King. Yet whereas the new King in 1965 was aloof while deeply respected, and inspired awe as the pinnacle of Tongan customary rank, Tu'ipelehake was approachable, open, generous hearted and jovial. His laughter was huge, infectious and uncomplex. His warmth and humanity were that of his mother. In this way at least, it was in Tu'ipelehake that she lived on in the perceptions of ordinary Tongans; for he too was loved by his people.

And then there was Tu'ipelehake's modesty, unexpected perhaps in one so well placed by birth and thus favoured at home and abroad. It never left him in spite of the preferments, the customary salutations, gifts and tributes – and limousines. In 1966, he was awarded an honorary CBE in the Queen's Birthday list of that year. We wrote from Fiji to congratulate him. He replied, using our Tongan names. (p. 145)

Twenty-five years later in February 1991, I called on an ailing Prime Minister after a meeting of the Privy Council. He had presided as Prince Regent in the absence of the King, who was in New Zealand. He held out his left hand to me as we met again after so long. The lines of strain on his face had deepened; the voice was high and faltering; the eyes wandered; the smile was pale and fleeting. But the warmth was still there. 'How good of you to come,' he said. We reminisced, but nothing of substance was possible. It seemed a great effort of will.

Greater still was the effort of his departure. Soldiers lifted him slowly and carefully. They steadied his slow stick-aided progress to the entrance to the chamber and gently helped him into HM2, the black limousine which waited outside. Another royal Polynesian sun was beginning to set on its distant horizon.

Flying foxes live in a great tree at Kolovai on Tongatapu. During the day, hundreds of these quarrelling creatures cling blindly and upside down to the branches. At night their black bodies surge querulously into the darkness. The Tongan belief is that if a white flying fox appears, it is as a harbinger of impending royal death. The time will come when we see if reality lives up to legend.

"Fatai",

Nuku'alofa,

TONGA.

26th August, 1966.

Dear Toluafe and Fonu,

It is good to hear from you and Fonu again. Thank you very much for your kind message regarding the Honour which Her Majesty Queen Elizabeth has bestowed on me. The award is very high indeed, yet it was a great surprise to me, as I cannot think of any accomplishment that I have done. However, I have accepted it with a very thankful heart.

'Ofa atu to you both and the children.

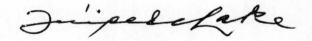

145

27

The Fanatic

'He is a Communist who should be hanged. And I'll be the first to string him up.' Thus spoke, reportedly, Minister of Police 'Akau'ola in the Nuku'alofa Club on his *bête noire*, 'Akilisi Pohiva: the man who, not unexpectedly in March 1991, proclaimed as one of his objectives the enforced resignation of the Minister of Police, backed by what he described as the first public motion in the history of Tonga seeking the removal of one of the King's ministers.

Speaker Fusitu'a of the Legislative Assembly was also in Pohiva's line of fire, judging by the headline, 'Speaker says "I will kill you"' (outside the House after a heated Assembly debate on money matters). This appeared in 'Akilisi's *Kele'a* news sheet for November to December 1990. Then there was his published pillorying of the Speaker for alleged unlawful access to and purchase of duty-free goods at Fua'amotu airport. Not unexpectedly, Fusitu'a was suing him for defamation. As in other places, the lawyers of Tonga are not idle.

'Akilisi Pohiva is the No. 1 People's Representative for Tongatapu. He topped the poll in the 1990 elections and for this reason alone, is not a man whom you can discount or brush aside.

'Eseta Fusitu'a was responsible for the Government's public relations activities. She works to Chief Secretary Taniela Tufui in the office of the Prime Minister. As she is also the wife of Noble and Speaker Fusitu'a, it was reasonable to assume that she would have views about 'Akilisi Pohiva so I asked her. This is what she said: 'In Pohiva we have Tonga's first fanatic. It is something new for us. The structure of our society and our inter-family links have together acted in the past as a constraint on extreme attitudes or actions. This is because of the effect these would have on our relatives with whom we live closely. Not so with Pohiva. There seems to be a burning resentment in him which prevails over all other considerations. He confronts the ministers and nobles in the Legislative Assembly, prods and probes on and on and ends up by angering and alienating them. Then he wonders why they do not support him. 'Afeaki, on the other hand, says much the same sort of thing, but he does so in more measured and persuasive terms. So he is more likely to be listened to by the nobles.'

It is easy to see why there is this perception. 'Akilisi *is* a confrontationalist and knows it. He is also without fear, although occasionally he may not be entirely without doubt. If so, it does not show. He knows how to exploit the English language: 'The whole central edifice is a crumbling catacomb of compromised corruption.' Though the substance might take some proving, this is not the language of concession or negotiation. Full frontal is his style and it is very un-Tongan. He cannot be ignored, nor will he go away. He is Tonga's first fulltime politician.

I thought of Robbie Burns' plaint from which the King quotes in his Foreword:

> O wad some Pow'r the giftie gie us
> To see oursels as others see us
> It wad frae mony a blunder free us . . .

So I went to see him.

'You have been described to me as a fanatic. How do you see yourself?'

'I don't consider myself to be a fanatic,' Pohiva replied, 'but I do have a burning (that word again) determination to put wrongs right. I am deeply concerned about the current situation in Tonga: corruption, scandals in Government and nepotism. We've been trying to get proper explanations from the Minister of Finance for ten years on matters that are unclear in the Estimates. We still do not get informative and accurate replies. All we get is more confusion. And there is no proper accountability by ministers of government to the people who provide the money through taxation.'

'Why are you as you are?'

'It is the way I was brought up, I suppose, in Ha'apai. I lost both my parents when I was very young and had to set out on life's struggle at too early an age. I had to learn fast to fend for myself. Things happened later which hardened me.' He smiled, a flicker only. The stress lines on his face relaxed momentarily and then returned.

Samuela 'Akilisi Pohiva was a pupil at Tupou College, then the Tonga Teachers' Training College, in 1962–3. He was a primary school teacher for ten years and won a scholarship to the University of the South Pacific in 1976–8. He emerged with a Bachelor of Education degree, much influenced, he says, and reinforced in his attitudes to life. He returned to the Teachers' Training College as a lecturer in 1979. Three years later he was 'removed' and seconded to a disaster-relief post following Hurricane Isaac in 1982. He returned to education administration only to be dismissed from the Civil Service by Cabinet in February 1985.

That dismissal was a watershed in his life; he considers it a short-sighted decision and is still unsure as to who made it. Pohiva received his dismissal notice on 22 February 1985. No reason was given. 'I talked to the Minister and could elicit no explanation. I wrote three separate letters to the Cabinet asking for the reasons and circum-stances of my dismissal. I received no reply to any of them. So I decided to take the Government to court for wrongful dismissal. It was a long battle, but I did not give up. It took me three years until I won the case in 1988 with $25,000 damages plus costs. The whole thing was declared to be at fault in both substance and procedure and in violation of clause seven of the Constitution: "It shall be lawful for all people to speak write and print their opinions and no law shall ever be enacted to restrict this liberty. There shall be free-dom of speech and of the press for ever . . ."

'I suppose it was sparked off by the private radio programme I had started in 1984. When I was dismissed, the programme was banned and that is how my paper *Kele'a* was born. They regret it all now, I think. I am able to be much more outspoken.'

'The essence of your objectives: what are they?'

'Oh quite simple, really. A ceremonial monarch, symbolic only; two houses of parliament like the British system and full democracy, of course; ministers fully accountable through the parliamentary system and not appointed by the monarch. The existing land system seems to be appropriate for Tonga and I would not want to change that fundamentally . . . We will see all these things. The process of liberation is on the way. We are having a demonstration on Friday 8 March to present a petition to the King against the recent amend-ments to the Constitution and seeking the removal of the Minister of Police.'

'I am afraid that I shall be in Vava'u.'

'Oh well. You can see a video of it . . .'

'. . . And the Crown Prince?'

'I have a feeling that Tonga doesn't need him. In a sense he is a foreigner. He seems to be bored in Parliament and very rarely speaks. I suppose that he has no time for the agenda items. You saw that he was in the House for the first day only of the February 1991 special session; and then the next day he was away out of Tonga again for weeks. But we have spoken frankly from time to time. I think that he perceives a great need for change in the upper levels of govern-ment and would support the introduction of a fully democratic electoral system. After all, if Western Samoa can do it (in April 1991) so should we in Tonga.'

'If I'd had to place a bet,' I said, 'on which of the two societies would have moved first, I believe that I would have chosen Samoa as the less likely to move. But they have, even though only *matais* can stand for their parliament.'

'We will do the same,' said Pohiva. 'We will not give up.'

'It has been suggested to me that you are a threat to stability in Tonga in that you will stop at nothing to achieve your objectives.'

Pohiva smiled. 'Everyone is entitled to an opinion.'

One other opinion I sought was that of Viliami 'Afeaki, whose contrasting tactical approach to matters of change and political infighting in the legislative chamber had been suggested by 'Eseta Fusitu'a. By chance, we dined together at the Paradise Hotel in Vava'u. He has a big round resonant voice that begins, deep down, within a big round body; but it has a gentleness when he speaks of family things. And family matters a great deal to him. He remembers with affection his father's example in the Legislative Assembly before him, and calls him 'Dad'. That is one arresting contrast with the family deprivations of 'Akilisi Pohiva.

Like his father before him – and initially against his father's advice – 'Afeaki went into the Tongan hustings and now represents the central group of islands, Ha'apai, in the Legislative Assembly. While in basic sympathy with the objectives and critical thrust of his colleagues on the benches of the People's Representatives, he finds himself increasingly out of sympathy with their tactics and approach. He is not a confrontationalist. He was born into a Roman Catholic family, but became a Mormon in 1972. His religious affiliations and his Church's approach to Tonga and to its establishment clearly influence his thinking. So too his twenty years in hotel business management in the United States.

'We need to work slowly in the Tongan way. I don't believe that Bishop Finau should have taken part in the march to the Palace on Friday. He should be aware, but aloof from dissent. Then he can counsel.'

That is not the approach, I remembered, of Anglican Archbishop Desmond Tutu, who has always been in the forefront of processional protest; but Bishop Finau would have parted company with Archbishop Tutu over the question of whether or not violent protest could ever be justified within the Christian faith.

'There has been a change in the last few years. Ministers are listening now. There is dialogue, individually. I never have any problem seeing a minister, and the appointment of a Government Information Officer is a step forward. I do not believe that the way ahead is through confrontation. 'Akilisi is consumed with bitter resentment, but it is difficult to tell what he wants to do.'

'What do you suggest for him?'

'Oh, I'd make him ombudsman. Outside Parliament. He'd be excellent at that. Parliament accepted a motion in 1988 to appoint an ombudsman, but nothing has happened.'

'Would he buy that?'

'I don't know. It's worth a try.'

'It is often a good idea to make a bad boy a prefect?'

'Yes. They can make the best.'

'If the right material is there from the beginning. You just have to remix the ingredients.'

'Afeaki thrust the knife into his pepper steak. 'I think George Tupou I knew a thing or two when he gave Tonga to God in 1862. I am sure He has a soft spot for this little country and will look after it.'

Blessed are the Tongans, I thought, with some biblical adaptation, for perhaps they have indeed inherited the earth. Their part of it, anyway.

28

A Voice from the Past

I spotted old Hale Vete walking with deliberation and a walking stick along Nuku'alofa's main street. He was a pioneer Tongan businessman and as such the owner of one of the first down-town – and down-market – cinemas or picture theatres as they were called in the Antipodes. This one was of heterogeneously ill-fitting timber construction and was largely unacquainted with paint. With but half a roof, it was a garage by day, a cinema by night. It then offered hard wooden backless benches and a wall-to-wall carpet of peanut shells.

Nothing has changed, close to half a century on. Today it is still there, held together, it seems, by paper and string and leased to some Taiwanese for undisclosed purposes.

'Hale,' I said. He was wearing one of the improbable singlets I remembered. I had never seen him wear a *ta'ovala*. 'Your cinema doesn't look a bit different after so many years.'

'Yes,' he replied. 'I'm rather proud of that.'

'But anywhere else, it would have had closure and demolition orders placed on it ages ago. One match would dispose of it in ten minutes.' I pointed to the scrap heap across the road. 'Why have you kept it like that?'

He looked at me in surprise and disbelief. 'There are so many modern buildings in Nuku'alofa now that I thought young people should know how things were in the past. So I am going to keep it like it is and to hell with everybody.'

He moved on, stick tapping, the obstinate independence of half a century ago still alive and kicking in his aged body.

29

A Voice from Within

'With the retirement of Tu'ipelehake as Prime Minister, I am the longest serving Cabinet minister. What greatly concerns me is the attitude of some of my colleagues towards the need for change.'

Thus, Dr Langi Kavaliku, one of His Majesty's Ministers, who lived then in the old 'rat-infested' residence of that one-night headmaster of Tonga College in 1954.

'As long ago as 1975, I put up specific proposals to His Majesty for constitutional change designed to give the people a greater voice in determining the course of their affairs while retaining and reinforcing the monarchy. It was debated in Cabinet at twelve separate meetings, deferred time after time and then dropped. The essence of my proposals is that Government must: become more efficient and caring and develop and maintain an image of responsibility and integrity; be more open and explain to the public what it is doing and why; aim to change to a fully elected system over a period of time – no less than nine nor more than fifteen years in a three-phrase development programme.

'Change, like race, is a fact of life,' says Kavaliku. 'Tonga must rethink and reshape its institutions and its ideas to retain what is best of Tonga while allowing the development of a system that meets rising and changing aspirations and needs. What emerges must be a system that is accepted by all sections of the Tongan community.

'Now, in 1991, sixteen years later, time may be running out. It is vital in my opinion that the Government take the initiative and announce a constitutional review. It should just accept the principle of examining these matters and start the process publicly. There are plenty of fundamental changes in Tongan history. The 1875 Constitution itself was a significant one. I would like an announcement about the setting up of a Royal Commission to be made by the King on the occasion of the twenty-fifth anniversary of his coronation on 4 July 1992, or even a year later when the King is seventy-five. If something like that is done, the Government will be seen at last to be adopting a positive approach. Not stagnating. But sometimes I don't know whether we can afford to wait that long.'

At fifty-one (at the time of our meeting), Langi Kavaliku is the youngest member of the Tongan Cabinet, apart from the Crown Prince. He is a commoner who went to Harvard, Cambridge and the London School of Economics. No mean achievement for anyone, let alone a humble academic disciple of his King. He became the first Tongan PhD. Immediately thereafter, in 1966, he was appointed, while still only twenty-six, as Minister Without Portfolio. It was an imaginative move, since he became acquainted early on with the business and proceedings of Cabinet without carrying premature ministerial responsibility for a specific subject. Twenty-five years on, he has the interesting but curious portfolio of Education, Works and Civil Aviation. Since September 1991, he is also Deputy Prime Minister.

'You are,' I said, 'a man of no little academic distinction and physical dimensions. It is an unusual combination.'

The responsive laughter, like the man, was rich in recognition of the human condition,.

'You are saying, are you not,' he said, 'that I am really a big fat fellow.'

The other special distinction of Langi Kavaliku is that he and his second wife have seventeen children, ranging in age from eighteen to thirty-two. All are adopted in the Polynesian way. Twelve live at home, two are in New Zealand and one each is in the United States, Japan and Australia. He has a whole Rugby team – or future government perhaps – in just one family.

'Tongan work ethics are so different in other countries,' says Dr Kavaliku. 'There they try noticeably harder. I have often wondered why this is. In my travels, I got sick of seeing Tongans washing dishes. So an undeclared objective of our education policy is to equip our young people with some skills or talents which will be of use to them wherever they choose to live in the modern world. You can read what you like into that, but I guess I seek to make something out of nothing.'

In one respect at least, the Minister of Education certainly succeeds. I had already met the surprisingly outspoken doctor of linguistics. One day the Minister was at his desk, a departmental official sitting opposite, when he spotted me through the open louvre windows.

'I want you to meet someone. Mana Latu, another of our Deputy Directors of Education.'

A man in his early fifties in tie, *vala*, and *ta'ovala* jumped to his feet and grasped my hand.

'Bain. I remember you sitting in the Premier's office. I used to come in to see the Director of Education, Mr Reid, and get my instructions. I was his houseboy.'

Tonga, as Pesi Fonua says, is where you learn to expect – and to accept – the unexpected.

'So now you are a Deputy Director of Education . . .' I looked for sensible words and did not find them. 'How wonderful to see you. Congratulations. Thank you, Minister. Don't let me interrupt your meeting any further.'

'You weren't interrupting. I invited you in. Far more interesting than what we have to deal with now.'

Back at the Friendly Islander, I sat down to my desk to try to write – battling with the heat and the humidity – now shirtless, in underpants and *vala*.

The room maid knocked and asked the equivalent in Tongan of 'Can I do you now, sir?'

'Of course. Please do. I shan't be going out.'

She picked up the wet towels, glanced reluctantly at last night's dishes, and in that deceptively innocent Tongan way, asked: 'Aren't you going to work today?'

'I am at work now.'

She looked disdainful, unbelieving. 'That's not work. You are just writing.'

Pat Matheson had been right. Again.

30

A Royal Bicycle Ride

'Be at Taufiva Stadium at five o'clock this afternoon,' the King had said. 'I do fifteen rounds. You can bring a photographer, if you wish.'

So we went, Pesi and I, in the late afternoon sun of an oppressive March day. The King arrived in HM1, klaxons blaring. He walked slowly through the entrance tunnel to the track. Rugby football practice in the centre came to a halt, and the players sank down on the pitch. In the presence of the monarch, they must be thus seated and still.

The King was dressed in a white stretch T-shirt, with 'Tui Vava'u' in large letters across the chest. On the back (tactfully, I thought) was the counterpart inscription, 'Tui Ha'apai'. He wore a blue sailor's cap, heavy dark goggles, brown shorts, white socks and white canvas boots. A bicycle stood waiting in the middle of the *en tous cas* track. It had a lavishly padded seat with wheels smaller than the standard size. A large red leather armchair stood empty beside it.

'So you came,' His Majesty called out when he saw me.

'Yes, with a photographer, as you kindly suggested.'

'This is an interesting grandstand,' said the King, pointing behind me. 'The French contractors ran out of money. They left five roof beams unfinished at each end which we have to complete. But it is a beautiful track and ground, as you can see. We in Tonga don't hate the French as so many countries seem to do.'

'That had not escaped my notice,' I said, remembering the King's acceptance of a French invitation to visit Muroroa Atoll when the rest of the South Pacific was seething with disapproval about the continuance of French nuclear testing.

'In my experience, they will be nice to you if you are not rude to them. So we are not rude to them. In such matters, Tonga is not the odd man out. It is the odd man in.' He smiled with satisfaction.

I thought once again what pragmatists the King and the Crown Prince are. In this respect at least they seem to be at one.

'Well. I must get started.' He dropped his two metal sticks, progressed to the bicycle and mounted it with the assistance of the assembled soldiery.

He set off anti-clockwise round the athletics track, accompanied by seven runners who handed over the baton of responsibility to their replacements every three rounds. Head down, he was total concentration. Two other cyclists paced the King from a discreet distance behind. A soldier stood on the steps of the stand holding a green metal flame thrower. With a spanner he clanged the number of circuits completed as the King and his runners went by. The soldier was clad in green khaki, black beret, white belt, white gaiters and boots. His smartness would have passed muster in Horse Guards Parade.

'You should have brought a bicycle and come with us,' said the King as he had started off.

Now that had not occurred to me. Just as well. The track is a circuit of 440 metres and the King clocks fifteen tollings of the flame thrower before he stops. It is a bravura achievement for someone of seventy-three years, when we were speaking, and carrying such weight.

'I told you this morning that I feel like a man of sixty. This sort of thing is why. Three times a week I do my rowing. The other two days I cycle here.'

As the King sank into the royal chair beside the track, the royal physician, Dr Tilitili Puloka, stepped up to take the royal pulse. 'One hundred and twenty,' said the King. 'You'll see it will be down to eighty in ten minutes. It used to take half an hour. Did you see my bicycle? It is a Taiwanese-built American mountain machine with eighteen speeds. I use the top gear so the bicycle does the work.'

Well, some of it, I thought. The effort of will and concentration is clearly considerable.

'I must get off home now,' said His Majesty. 'I have some food, a massage, a bath and then a wonderful sleep. My muscles are perfect for fifteen laps. I used to do eighteen, but it made me stiff next day.'

The soldiers raised the King to his feet. He walked across the track and, with a portable wooden step to assist, clambered back into HM1. Two royal grandchildren had watched in wonderment from the rear window. Unknown to them then, they were being given memories to treasure.

'In 1976,' said the royal physician, 'the King's weight was a serious problem. I think it was 444 pounds at that time. Now we have it down to about 350.'

'And the wheezing,' I said, 'which he used to suffer from the slightest exertion seems to have vanished?'

'Totally.'

The King's cycling pacers were Ralph Sanft and Albin Johanssen, both from old settler families, intermarried with Tongans. Sanft has retail businesses and is the honorary German consul in Tonga. Johanssen runs his own accounting firm and is the honorary Swedish consul.

'And what,' I asked them, 'is the motivation?'

They looked at each other and smiled. 'Longevity.'

Yes, I thought. That is it; the example is before him of the father of modern Tonga, King George Tupou I, who died in 1893 at the age of ninety-six after a reign of forty-eight years. Plus the approach of the twenty-first century.

Tonga could be about to experience another historically long reign, this time by a sovereign with the compelling urge to survive and thus to prevail . . . To prevail, I wondered, over what? Infirmity? Change? The inexorable destiny with death? Perhaps it was a kind of spiritual nobility. Shakespearean. Maybe I would find out.

'On Tuesday,' the King said, 'I row. At Faua wharf. The inner harbour. Four o'clock. You should come there too.'

Now that, I thought, will present difficulty. I had asked the Queen a few days before whether she would consider choosing a *tapa* design for the cover of this book, as Her Majesty had done in 1966 for *The Friendly Islanders*.

'Yes,' the Queen said on Saturday afternoon at the residential palace at Fua'amotu. 'There is a special *tapa* designed by Queen Salote herself for (her granddaughter) Princess Pilolevu. It has not been otherwise used so far as I know. I'll get one of the Palace women to get it out so that you can see it. I'll be in town for a meeting on Tuesday. Come to the Palace in Nuku'alofa at, say, four o'clock. They can cut you a piece.'

So I attempted for the first and assuredly the last occasion to keep two royal assignations at the same time. The Palace first. The rear gates were open ready but not for me. First a land cruiser with soldiers, the royal standard flying above both front mudguards. Then two uniformed motor cyclists surged through and, at precisely four p.m., the great Chevrolet Silverado land cruiser, HM1, with the King inside. The gates were closed again. I drove to the resident sentry in PM25, which ought to have been good enough, but wasn't.

'I have an appointment with Her Majesty Queen Mata'aho at four o'clock.'

Maybe he was accustomed to that sort of presumed *laupisiness* from tourists. He gazed unblinking at me with what I can only describe as the look of a not so friendly New Friendly Islander. PM25 did not seem to register or to matter if it did.

'What do you want to talk to her about?' he eventually asked.

Replies like 'none of your business' and 'get lost' suggested themselves and were sensibly rejected. Had he asked the Queen's mother that sort of question when she was once refused entry to the *tapu* grounds of the Palace when she attempted to see her daughter? India's great cricketer, Sunil Gavaskar, was similarly turned away at the Grace Gates of Lord's Cricket Ground in London with dire consequences, when the MCC invited him to accept honorary life membership. No thanks, said Gavaskar huffily, and went on his way.

As it happened, the Queen had been called elsewhere. She had left instructions about the *tapa* with her women, but not, apparently, with the Palace guard. It took the intervention of a committee of six, including the cheerful Acting Chief Inspector of Police, Mekita Pale, who is the Queen's personal security attendant and lady-in-waiting. With a mixture of firmness and persuasion, she sorted things out so that in the end I was permitted to walk some thirty yards inside to the old Palace office. A great swathe of royal *tapa* lay spread across the lawn.

'The Queen told me to cut a piece for you,' said one of the attendants. I marvelled at this potential mutilation of what was special *tapa* of some thirty-five years. But the cut was neat and the roll more than large enough for the choice of the section for the design.

The sentry glowered as I set off for Faua wharf, leaving for the King and Queen a video from Margaret of an international art exhibition she had organised in Fiji in March 1987. Princess Pilolevu had been guest of honour. It seemed appropriate in a way.

As with the royal Tongan cycling, royal rowing is like none other. It is a solitary and mass exercise, all at the same time. The King rows alone, but a well-manned power-boat follows the royal water progress at close distance. The skiff he uses is Australian-built, fifteen feet or so in length. A three-foot pole is mounted in the stern with a large mirror on top so that the King can see where he is heading without looking round. With his weight, that would be hazardous, so the head stays down; as with the cycling, eyes intent on oars, hands and legs.

Getting the King aboard involved twenty soldiers, police and boatmen. From HM1, the King walked slowly down a slipway to the edge of the water where a more substantial boat was positioned. A series of hands and counter-balancing bodies ladled the King after a fashion across the first boat and slowly down on to the seat of the royal skiff. When he was settled, the King positioned himself a few yards offshore and waited for his entourage to assemble in the following boat. In or with it were ten soldiers, oarsmen, swimmers and, once again, the royal doctor.

The King accomplished three lengths – 1,200 metres, he says – in twenty careful minutes. The swimmers sprang into the warm waters of the harbour and gently directed the skiff to the landing place. Then followed the reverse procedure for disembarkation. His Majesty did not tarry. The sun had been hot, the effort considerable. All that had been missing was Handel and his Water Music. Maybe one day the King's own brass band might use his transcription from the original.

On the prow of the skiff, in bold lettering, was 'Nestlé Milo'.

'Nothing to do with me,' said the King, when I asked him. 'It was there when I got it.'

Yes, I thought, it just came with the bus, as 'Alone had said.

31

A Tale of Two Passports

It all appears to have started in 1982 and 1983 when amendments to Tonga's Passport Act were passed. They introduced the concept of a 'Tonga Protected Person', a non-Tongan who, subject to certain conditions and upon payment of a prescribed fee, was eligible to apply for a Tonga Protected Person passport. This passport, which did not confer citizenship or the right to residence in Tonga, was essentially a document of convenience for international travel. The proposition for such an arrangement, in respect of which Tonga is not alone among Pacific island countries, was apparently put to the King by a plausible Chinese businessman and targeted at Hong Kong Chinese who were looking gloomily at the end of British colonial rule and the return of the Colony to mainland China in 1997. The honorary consulate for Tonga in Hong Kong became the distribution centre for the issue of these passports. A fee of T$10,000 was payable and the demand, according to a statement by Minister of Police 'Akau'ola in a radio broadcast on 18 February 1991, 'was high. However, a serious impediment to the development of this programme was the increasing reluctance of some countries to recognise the Tonga Protected Person passport, because neither nationality nor the right of residence in Tonga was thereby conferred.' Understandable reluctance, you might conclude.

'To accommodate these increasing problems,' the Minister went on, 'the introduction of further legislation was anxiously considered by the Privy Council and Cabinet, resulting in the passing by His Majesty and the Legislative Assembly of the Nationality (Amendment) Act 1984. The intention of this legislation was to confer upon His Majesty the additional power to grant letters of naturalisation to any foreigner of good character upon humanitarian grounds, subject to the imposition of conditions and limitations as he, in his discretion, might deem necessary to impose. The fee prescribed for the issue of naturalisations issued pursuant to the Act of 1984 was considerably higher and it was therefore envisaged that such applicants would also be persons with sound financial resources, who, when acquiring citizenship, would contribute financially and otherwise to the development of Tonga . . .'

The King was empowered without fetter or accountability to approve the naturalisation of non-Tongans and the consequent issue to them of ordinary Tongan passports. But the price to applicants 'of good character upon humanitarian grounds' was indeed high; and it seemed to many, perhaps unfairly, that humanitarian considerations would apply only to those who could afford to pay for their exercise. It was widely rumoured that one international figure in this category was the hard-pressed President Marcos of the Philippines whose international reputation was declining at the time. In April 1991, the Philippines press reported that his widow Imelda had obtained Tongan naturalisation. She denied this next day in Honolulu.

In February 1988, however, the Legislative Assembly was faced with an 'opposition' motion which sought to repeal the 1984 amending Act on the grounds that it was unconstitutional. Why? Because section 29 of the Constitution makes it clear that before letters of naturalisation can be approved, a prescribed minimum of five years' residence in Tonga must be fulfilled.

'Yes,' concluded the Attorney-General, 'this seems to be right. The constitutional position in this respect must have been overlooked in 1984. We had better repeal the amending Act of 1984 for Naturalisation on Humanitarian Grounds.' So this was duly done by the Nationality (Amendment) Act of 1988.

And that, you might have thought, would be that. But you would have been wrong. Between 1984 and 1988 a substantial number of non-Tongans had acquired naturalisation, principally through the Hong Kong office. They were now holders of ordinary Tongan passports and accordingly possessed the right of residence. Furthermore, the Hong Kong consulate appeared not to have been notified of the 1988 repeal; or, if it were notified, apparently took no notice because, as the Minister of Police announced, 'the majority of the naturalisations issued through the Hong Kong consulate were issued after the repeal of the Act of 1984 and in any event there were serious departures from the statutory procedures required to be followed.'

The total number of persons who had received ordinary passports which were now of doubtful validity was officially declared to be 426, all of them residing outside Tonga.

The Minister's statement continued:

The situation generally in relation to all persons who have acquired naturalisations and ordinary passports has become a matter of the gravest concern to His Majesty's Government and the anxieties grow daily. Such persons acquired what was understood to be full Tongan citizenship; they did so in good faith and the sums paid by them for the privilege have contributed substantially to the revenues of Tonga. The periods during which they have held their ordinary passports, and therefore the belief that they enjoyed full citizenship, vary between about five years and eighteen months. Moreover, many of these persons would, or might, be rendered stateless if they were deprived of their apparent Tongan nationalities and passports. During the present period of uncertainty, however, the Ministry of Police has felt itself unable to service the apparently legitimate and very pressing requirements of increasing numbers of such persons, for the renewal or replacement of passports, or to issue passports to children who have been born into their families. An immediate solution to this intolerable state of affairs must, therefore, be found.

His Majesty's Government acknowledges that serious legal difficulties exist in relation to all passports which were issued or purportedly issued in pursuance of the Act of 1984, but is wholly satisfied, having regard to all the circumstances, that it must act urgently to protect the innocent holders thereof by taking decisive steps to put their positions beyond legal doubt. Apart from Tonga's undoubted moral obligations in the matter, the legal consequences to the individuals concerned, of their passports being declared invalid, would be wholly unacceptable to them and also highly prejudicial to the interests of the country.

So in the absence of the King who had gone to New Zealand for his annual medical check-up, his brother Prince Tu'ipelehake, as Prince Regent, summoned the Legislative Assembly to a special session at ten a.m. on Monday 18 February 1991. Within the corridors of Tongan power, the ministers of government were far from united as to the wisdom of the decision to call the Assembly together at this time. One minister felt so strongly about the untimeliness of throwing the whole matter open to parliamentary debate and thus public examination that he announced to his colleagues his intention of remaining silent throughout the debate. And this he did, until close to the end.

You might not think that the issue of special categories of passports to anxious Orientals by a government supposedly seeking to increase its store of foreign exchange reserves would divide the country or call into question the probity and integrity of its monarch and ministers. Yet court proceedings were instituted to establish the defectiveness, illegality or constitutional impropriety of the Government's actions in this respect, which provoked it to emerge from its customary quiescence and to adopt frantic defensive measures, including the engagement of an expensive British QC to advise how best the Government might disentangle itself from legal and procedural coils of its own making. Stranger still, perhaps, a special session of Parliament had to be summoned when normally only one annual (mid-year) sitting is held, purely for the purpose of enacting amendments to both the Constitution and the appropriate statute or law in order to put right, retrospectively, what had gone wrong and so frustrate the court action by pre-empting the questions for judicial decision.

The public perception, justified or not, of what happened in Tonga in February 1991 was that it was for those reasons and those reasons alone that the Legislative Assembly was, exceptionally, called together. It was these sittings which I attended in the February heat, generated not only by the heavy and humid weather, but by the increasing tension as the debate wound on and the frustrations of the Representatives of the People deepened. Not least were the official benches aware, as everyone well knew, that the man who initiated the proceedings which challenged the Government in the court building but a few yards away from that of the Legislative Assembly, was the same man, 'Akilisi Pohiva, No. 1 Representative for Tongatapu, who carried much of the burden of the argument against the Government in the parliamentary debate.

The Attorney General and Minister of Justice, David Tupou, opened the batting for the Government. He explained why the Assembly had been urgently recalled; he set out the issues broadly as contained in the statement of the Minister of Police; and he urged Honourable Members to support the proposed amending legislation as a straightforward and unencumbered solution to the Government's current difficulties. Only then would Tonga's good name be restored internationally.

It was a good try, but he did not succeed in achieving a technical knock-out in the first round. I doubt if he thought that he could. The problems – and opportunities they offered to serious and determined critics – were not to be resolved so readily.

And there was another factor which lay in the essence of three short sentences in section 41 of the Constitution of Tonga:

The King is the Sovereign of all the Chiefs and all the people. The person of the King is sacred. He governs the country but his ministers are responsible.

The questions began to fly thick and fast to the Attorney General: how much has the Government of Tonga received for these passports? Where is it? What has it been used for? Who is responsible for its day-to-day management? Can we have an itemised statement of receipts and expenditure? Was the Hong Kong office advised to terminate the issue of passports or was it not? Where are the accounts kept? Have they been audited and, if so, by whom? Why has the House not been informed of these things? Why is it not informed now? Can we please have the figures? Why are they not available? And so on. And so on.

They were penetrative but foreseeable questions, all a bit beyond the duty of an Attorney General to answer. So 'Akau'ola, Minister of Police, took a hand and across the floor faced his adversary 'Akilisi Pohiva, whose central objective soon became clear: the Minister's dismissal or resignation. The King would escape but some of the mud might stick.

'Why don't you ask me?' asked 'Akau'ola. 'I am Minister of Police and as such I am the minister responsible for the issue in Tonga of Tongan passports.'

It did not appear to make much difference. The Representatives of the People failed over five days and three evenings to extract informative answers to their probing questions. Especially on the matter of money. 'Akilisi Pohiva was angered by the fact that while Tongan critical oratory was in full emotive flight, 'Akau'ola sat calmly reading the latest edition of *Time* magazine and its cover story on the progress of the Gulf War.

Acting Prime Minister Baron Vaea, the Alfred Tupou of No. 6 New Zealand squadron, took a navigating hand. The essence of his intervention was that the Government was merely seeking to put right and thus re-legalise what had become unlawful. There was nothing wrong or improper in doing that, retrospectively. Indeed, the Government had a duty to do it. There was no conflict with section 20 of the Constitution which says:

> It shall not be lawful to enact any retrospective laws in so far as they may curtail or take away or affect rights or privileges existing at the time of the passing of such laws.

What the proposals before the House were designed to do, Vaea repeated, was to legalise and legitimise the past beneficial consequences of the Government's wholly acceptable intentions . . .

Well, that is how I rationalised it at the time. It too was a good try.

The Minister of Finance sat largely silent, if uneasy. His interventions were minimal and inexplicit. The reasons were obvious, if unstated.

In July 1989, the Legislative Assembly had passed the Tonga Trust Fund Act. This provided for the management of moneys segregated from the ordinary revenues of Government to be used to fund development projects approved by the Legislative Assembly. Audited reports were to be laid before it. The Trustees were the Prime Minister, the Attorney General and the Minister of Finance.

But why so? And what was to be in this Fund? You've guessed it: none other than the proceeds from the passport scheme, stashed away in a California bank account. 'Royal family pocket money, it is widely assumed,' a cynical Governor of the Reserve Bank said to me. Guesses about the amount in the fund ranged from two to three times the figure of $14 million given by the King in the *Chronicle* newspaper a year before, reportedly for the protected-person passport programme alone! Whatever the figure, the objective of the trust fund was clear: to keep the money away from the ordinary budgetary and foreign exchange processes and rules of government. It says something about the perceived role and status of the Legislative Assembly which should be, but apparently is not, the final arbiter for the control and authorised expenditure of public revenues, irrespective of their source.

Nevertheless, even if the legislative body were that final arbiter, its judgment and decisions would not be of significance when its current membership means that it is weighted so heavily against full public accountability. 'The Tonga Legislative Assembly is just a rubber stamp for the Government,' Papiloa Foliaki had said in Fiji at an early stage in her parliamentary experience. Whether this is strictly so or not, the fact remains that there is no Public Accounts Committee.

So the debate proceeded and the people of Tonga learned about what was happening on their front doorstep from Radio Australia news bulletins. Radio Tonga was silent on the subject throughout the sitting. 'Speaker Fusitu'a issued instructions that we were not to broadcast anything,' they said in their defence of the apparently indefensible. 'Not so,' said Fusitu'a, whose wife 'Eseta is, as you already know, the nearest thing to a government information officer, 'I gave no such instructions.' Which is Tonga all over. Truth is still relative, not absolute. The new Friendly Islanders are in this respect not perceptibly different from the old.

At the end of the week the legislation with the amendment to the Constitution had been passed, as had always been likely, since the

Representatives of the Nobles, who spoke but briefly and intermittently in the debate, voted as usual with the Government. By mutual agreement, the court case was abandoned with substantial concessional costs awarded to Pohiva. The Attorney General and his imported Queen's Counsel celebrated appropriately in the Nuku'alofa Club. So did Pohiva elsewhere and for different reasons.

Not so Papiloa with whom I spoke next day. Her mood was sombre. There was nothing for her to celebrate, it seemed. Teacher, nurse, doctor's wife and pioneer businesswoman, she now owns and runs the twelve-year-old Friendly Islander, a sort of family motel a little way along the Nuku'alofa coastal road from the International Dateline Hotel. There is no similarity between the two, and none either between Papiloa and Tongan women you pass in the street. Papiloa Foliaki was the first elected woman commoner in Tonga's Legislative Assembly from 1978–81. There has been none since.

'It was the best education I ever had. I learned about the law, about royalty, about the Government, and so on . . . The same people were in the Privy Council, the Cabinet and the Legislative Assembly. I thought that the balance of representation in the Assembly was not fair. I agree with the King still appointing the Ministers, but he should appoint some of the elected Representatives of the People as Ministers. He could do that without any amendment to the Constitution. It is long overdue. If there is no authority, there is no power. I have come to realise that the people have the ultimate power, and that is what worries me now about what the present Representatives of the People are doing. If you motivate the minds of the people, that is the most powerful area. I hope and pray our leaders will come to realise that. It is very dangerous to play with the power of the mind, and frightening too.

'That is what they are doing now. A few agitators are waking up the people and saying that they have been used for a long time. Seeds of doubt are being spread in the minds of the people. They are saying that money is the weakness of this society, and that the people have been misused to create anxiety and make them believe that they have been cheated. If the Government does not counteract all this, it will go on happening. For my part, I am very concerned about this indoctrination . . .'

I thought it time to ask a question. 'Are you saying that there is a systematic attempt to undermine, if not destroy, public confidence in the Government and its institutions?'

'Yes,' she said, 'it has become a revolution of the mind. Once you revolt in your mind, the rest follows. Like Hitler. Once the seeds were planted, everyone believed and followed him. When Tongans are poor, they know who they are and how to behave. But now economic change has brought a change in status and thus disharmony. Everyone is trying to get "the most dollar". Commercialism and tradition are now in conflict, even in the monarchy itself. In commerce, everyone is the same. Ordinary people are saying, "If the monarchy is doing what we are doing, what are we to do? What is behind our royalty any more? It is bringing in foreigners." The people prefer the *papalangi*. They were here before the Chinese. Ordinary people fear that no one is caring for them; therefore you have to fight for favours and this leads to corruption. Now we are nothing, nobodies. There is mistrust in the Government, which is not concerned about us any more. They only care about themselves and their relatives and friends. This area of self-respect has gone. In the past the Tongans felt proud. Now they feel degraded.'

The telephone erupted. There was a flow of Tongan followed by English. Some bookings for the tourist season soon to begin. It was a good sign, provided it lasted. She turned to me, face serious and concerned again.

'The Government acted to make right a wrong while the court case was pending. The Constitution says that there is one law for all. Now it is not so any longer. We have seen wrongs righted for the nobility because they have the power. When the people do wrong, there is no way the law will be amended to put right their wrong.' She paused and sighed. 'For those of us who support the present system in Tonga, the hurt is the greatest.'

'Do you foresee violence?' I asked.

'Yes. That man [I assumed she meant Pohiva] will stop at nothing until he has overthrown the system and he is in power. He is the mouthpiece for a group which is not in Parliament. It is all so complex. The Constitution says that the person of the King is sacred. But if he comes down to the marketplace of business and profit-and-loss accounts, he is competing with the people – unfairly. The two things are not compatible.'

Papiloa smiled a sad smile. 'All this is why "the passport" is very dangerous. It is an arrow in the heart of the people.'

32

The King

The sheer bulk of the man, the quintessence of Tongan nobility in stature, is the first inescapable visual impression. Hence the cliché, none the less true: the largest king of the smallest kingdom. After that, gradually to the stranger comes the recognition that weightiness lies also in the mind and his perceptions of human behaviour both in his own land and beyond. In his presence, no reminder is necessary that Tonga is the only remaining Polynesian kingdom and he its monarch.

'It is the sovereign,' he says, 'who is the guardian of popular leadership in Tonga, not parliament. The Tongan monarchy has a tradition of liberalism. I like to think of myself as the head of a monarchical democracy.' It is a historically understandable conceit, but not one which is entirely persuasive in the harsh realities of the late twentieth century.

For forty-four years, Taufa'ahau has presided over his country's policies: first as Premier for sixteen years, and then as King, on the death of his mother, Queen Salote Tupou III in 1965. The developmental and technological changes in the span of his reign are there for all to see. Custom and traditional social practices have had to struggle to survive. The fatal impact is not confined to the nineteenth century. For an island state in a shrinking world, not only inflation is imported.

Queen Salote gave birth to her first child at the Palace in Nuku'alofa on 4 July 1918. She was barely eighteen and had become wife, queen and mother in less than ten months. Her son was christened Siaosi Taufa'ahau Tupoulahi. The name was given by the royal child's grandfather, King George Tupou II, long before birth.

'When my mother, Queen Salote, was about three months pregnant,' the King told me, 'her father placed his hand on my mother's stomach and said: "It is a boy. You will have a son." And he thereupon gave the name which I was to have at birth. Accordingly,' and the King laughed, 'no provision was made at the Palace against the possible eventuality that the baby might turn out to be a girl. Well, it didn't and I wasn't.'

In the tiny royal child, those three ancient lines of Tongan kings

– the Tuʻi Tonga, the Tuʻi Haʻatakalaua and the Tuʻi Kanokupolu
– came together for the first time thus conferring unprecedented
customary status. The sovereign is the repository and the pillar of
custom and tradition: not easy for a king so commercially innovative
as Taufaʻahau was to become.

Semi-divine status attaches to the royal personage. Even his
immediate family comply with strict requirements of protocol,
behaviour, dress and speech. Indeed, there is a special royal language
and vocabulary for addressing the King and none other. The Palace
grounds are *tapu* and in the past would not be entered lightly. Now
there is that encircling security wall.

The royal prince was educated initially in Nukuʻalofa. He then
went to Newington College in Sydney. Thereafter, he graduated in
Arts and Law at the University of Sydney – the first Tongan to do
so. When he returned home from the freedoms of Australian life,
custom and rank confined him. He preferred to speak and think in
English, and he was impatient of the protracted ceremonial occasions
over which he was obliged to preside. It was Queen Salote who
taught him forbearance and gave him the knowledge which led to
understanding that if the people were obliged to wait upon their
future King, he in turn was obliged to wait for them, if only to catch
up. Coming to terms with this was to be his salvation.

He was twenty-five in 1943 when he was appointed by his mother
to be her Minister for Health and Education. In 1949, he became
Premier. The Queen bestowed upon him the royal title Tupoutoʻa
Tungi – broadly the Tongan equivalent of the Prince of Wales. In
his fifteen years as Premier and later Prime Minister, he was enter-
prising but inclined to be aloof: animated when conversation aroused
his interest, dull and unresponsive at times when it did not. His
attention span in Cabinet could be short. More often his judgment
and will prevailed. He chafed, even then, at the financial constraints
of government. When an item on the agenda involved the provision of money, the Cabinet decision could be unpredictable; if he
wanted something agreed, his view would be accepted even if the
Minister of Finance were to oppose it, albeit for good reason. If the
Premier were uninterested in the issue, the opinion of the Minister
of Finance was likely to determine the outcome ('for that was what
he was there for, was he not, to decide such matters?') and a huge
volley of royal laughter would follow such a grand concession to
consensus.

In a joint royal wedding ceremony in 1947 with his younger
brother, Prince Tuʻipelehake, the Crown Prince married Halaevalu

Mata'aho 'Ahome'e. She bore him three sons and one daughter. As Princess and Queen, Mata'aho has devoted her life to his care and support and to many social causes with which she has been closely identified. She has been his eyes and ears in the community, and has worked selflessly in its service. The debt to her is immense.

When Queen Salote died in 1965, there were many like 'Akau'ola who believed that an era of stability and benign guardianship of the integrity of Tongan life had come to an end. The new King was respected, not loved. And no one expected him to live as long as he has. His father and grandfather had died early. His great body weight made it seem unlikely that he would survive his biblical span. But in the last decade or so, and until the matter of passports and its possible implications, he appeared to grow closer to the people and they to him. His engaging eccentricities, like his bicycle rides and rowing, may in part explain this. In part only, because as we have seen there are perceived aberrations from within the royal church of latter-day complaints.

The 180th meridian of longitude passes through the Fiji Island of Taveuni. Tonga is 400 miles to the east of Taveuni, and should accordingly have been in the western hemisphere. This would not do for the people of Tonga, Taufa'ahau had early concluded. He decreed that, geography notwithstanding, the 180th meridian would be stretched sufficiently eastwards to embrace his kingdom and thus enable Tongan time to be thirteen hours ahead of Greenwich instead of eleven hours behind it. It is always a quiet satisfaction to the King that his people are the first in the world to greet the new day.

Enduring enjoyment lies too in the abacus to which he became attracted at an early age. His musical interests are wide-ranging and eclectic. He has encouraged choir competitions and transposed music, notably Handel and Bach, for his brass band and choir, both of which enjoy active royal patronage. He was, I used to think, a bit of an intellectual dilettante, widely read in a variety of subjects, superficially knowledgeable about many, yet at times disconcertingly erratic with those whose task it was to respond to and follow up his passionate but sometimes passing enthusiasms.

In the 1970s, the King's occasional susceptibility to gimmickry led him to endorse proposals for the introduction of peel-off sticker-type postage stamps, shaped like the fruit they represented. The philatelic reputation of Tonga plummeted and it was easy to understand why it began to be described as a 'banana monarchy'. Easy, but a little unfair. No one can be right all the time, not even a king, as some events in 1991 may have indicated.

King Taufa'ahau was in London in late October 1990 en route to Germany. He walked heavily with the aid of two sticks. I remarked when I saw him how his twenty-five-year reign had seen his South Pacific island fiefdom pass from the town crier to the satellite dish.

'Yes,' he said with delight, 'I have just ordered one for the Palace in Nuku'alofa. It is being shipped from Seattle now. I shall be a regular watcher of CNN.'

'And your visit to Germany?' I asked.

'I shall be the first Head of State to visit united Berlin. Over 130 years ago, Tonga had an understanding with Bismarck and provided coaling stations for German ships. It was before our Treaty of Friendship with Britain. Germany was a South Pacific colonial power in Samoa and New Guinea until 1919. There is thus some historic significance in my going there now, I suppose. In fact the Germans cannot help us enough. You have seen the foreshore. That was German and Japanese money. It has transformed the appearance of Nuku'alofa. The Germans have built a technical school where we are training sailors and ship's engineers and cooks.'

There was no procedural confusion about my visit to the Palace in Nuku'alofa for an audience with the King. Queen Mata'aho had arranged it and all the right instructions had been given. Maybe it had helped that His Royal Highness Prince Lavaka had, from his office in the Tonga Defence Force headquarters at Vilai Barracks, telephoned the Palace office before I left him to check that all was well. 'It is,' he told me. 'They are waiting for you.'

I was met outside the entrance by a courteous young uniformed aide-de-camp. As I walked across the sacred grounds of the Palace lawns for the first time since 1956, there was one pleasurable recollection and one sadness. The recollection was of appearing there for the cameras with Queen Salote just before the first royal visit of Queen Elizabeth and the Duke of Edinburgh thirty-eight years before in December 1953. The sadness was that the royal chapel is no more. Its roof was so badly damaged by Hurricane Isaac in 1982 that repairs were considered to be financially impracticable and the building was demolished. A century of historic royal ceremonial went with it. The gracious white wooden Palace looks a little bare now, and the old symmetry has gone.

Dressed informally, the King was sitting in a room cluttered with boxes and technical gadgetry. The morning of 18 March 1991 was oppressive. A fast-flow fan cooled him. He waved to me to remove my jacket and tie. Set out before him on a low table was a roll of design and construction plans.

'Yes, yes. Do sit down,' he said without preamble, 'I want to show you these. They are my main current preoccupation: the plans of an oil harbour for discharging crude oil into a refinery to be built at Hihifo, right at the end of this island. Now, have a good look at this. There will be two entrances with depths to seventy feet. Extra industrial areas will enable us to generate enough electric power to supply the whole of Tonga.'

'Is this dependent in any way on the discovery of economically exploitable oil reserves in Tonga?'

'No. This will be exclusively Middle-Eastern oil for our refinery. We have the firm agreement of Saudi Arabia to allocate us a hundred thousand barrels a day whenever we get this built.' The King looked down again at his plans. 'We can refine only fifty thousand barrels a day, so we will sell the rest of the crude. We will distribute throughout the South Pacific – French Polynesia, the Cook Islands, Fiji, the Solomons, Samoa, and so on. One of the big advantages is that we will have very cheap asphalt to do our roads; asphalt is an end product of the refinery.'

'Whose idea was this?'

'Mine.' The King chuckled.

'When did you have it?'

'I have had it for a long time. I have some oil traders in Texas. The principal figure is an Iranian, who is the son of the oil minister of Iran under the Shah. When the Shah got thrown out, the oil minister got thrown out too and the son became a crude-oil trader in America. He knows how to handle supplies of crude. He speaks Arabic as well as Farsi, so he is an ideal agent to talk with Middle-east sources.'

'And the question of funding?'

'There are several possible sources. It may be the World Bank, but a group of investors from Taiwan are impressed in a big way. The idea has yet to be approved in principle by the Government. Then we will seek the capital to put into it, get the engineers, and so on. The whole thing springs from the fact that the transportation costs of the finished product are so high. Distribution tankers of a thousand tons come here now from Australia, Singapore and Fiji. The crew for such vessels is the same as that for a two hundred thousand ton tanker . . .'

'You must be very glad that the Gulf War is over.'

'Yes. Of course. All this will transform the economy.'

'When do you think that the first refined oil will flow?'

'Construction completed and ready to run in two years.' The King smiled in anticipatory pleasure. 'We will open the refinery in 1993, I hope. On my seventy-fifth birthday.' I recalled the Crown Prince's words: 'What most people don't know about my father is that he was greatly affected by the depression in the 1930s. It is basically why he has consistently sought to develop Tonga and to diversify its economy.'

It was time to turn to more personal matters, ones of some delicacy. I had the royal physician's figures of that imponderable but ever-present question: the King's body weight.

'You have become a bit of a fitness fanatic. How much weight do you think you have lost?'

'Must be more than a hundred pounds.'

'What was your weight before?'

'Over four hundred pounds.'

'Do you feel better?'

'Of course.'

'You gave up alcohol, didn't you?'

'Yes. When I got married. And tobacco.'

'Unlike the President of Fiji, for example.'

'And he also eats bully-beef, which I don't.'

'What do you eat?'

'Normally roast beef and sometimes lamb.'

'Do you enjoy a lot of fish?'

'Yes. Especially smoked fish with white sauce. I have just been sent some from New Zealand.'

'I think it would be true to say that in 1965 when you came to the throne, there were many who believed then that it would not be a long reign.'

'They have since died.' The King shook with laughter. One of his engaging foibles is that he laughs loudly and happily at his own royal jokes. Nobody in Tonga minds, of course, although they seem to where I live. I have often wondered why. If the perpetrator does not rejoice in his own humour, then who else will?

'So you are on the way to emulating King George Tupou I who lived until he was ninety-six. Is that your wish, your objective? So far as you can control your own destiny?'

'That's right.'

'What was the dominant impression left upon you by your mother?'

'She was a very loving mother. When I went away to school, she wrote to me every week. During the whole of my schooling in Australia, my father wrote me about four letters in ten years.'

'Your mother wrote in Tongan, of course?'

'Yes.'

'This helped to keep alive your thinking through the medium of Tongan when all the time you were surrounded by English?'

'That is so. But I never had any problems with the Tongan language. I never forgot it.'

'What was the main guidance she sought to leave with you for the future?'

'A strong religious faith.'

'And a belief in tradition?'

'Oh yes, of course.'

Thus perhaps it was that in November 1991 the King and Queen embarked upon a visit to Israel en route to Italy and England. Jerusalem is the confluence of three world religions: Christianity, Judaism and Islam. And, some have said, it is none the better for that. The Church of the Holy Sepulchre enshrines what is believed to be the tomb of Christ and the site of the crucifixion on Calvary. The historic antagonisms and rivalry between the intendants – Greek Orthodox, Armenian, Russian Orthodox, Roman Catholic – are such that the keys of the great door are held by a non-Christian. Riots in the nave have not been unknown, not least at the Easter ceremony of Searching for the Holy Fire.

Israeli security ensured that there were no disturbances when the King and Queen of Tonga entered the church. Thereafter they journeyed on the biblical route north to Galilee. They sailed out over the waters of New Testament fishermen Simon and Peter; stood where the Sermon on the Mount is judged to have been delivered; and were baptised by total immersion in the River Jordan at the hands of an American Baptist minister who had flown from the United States for the purpose.

'My baptismal gown was specially sewn in Tonga,' the King told me a week or so later in London. 'Now it will be put away at the Palace in Nuku'alofa and only used for the same purpose in the future by my sons and daughter. It was, of course, an intriguing experience. The whole ceremony was televised by Israeli TV. I understand that I am the first head of state and king to be baptised there. Queen too, I suppose. Maybe it will establish a trend . . .'

'. . . Do you sometimes think back to that tragic occasion when you and Queen Mata'aho were flying to your dying mother's bedside in Auckland in December 1965? Your flight from Fiji was delayed and you did not arrive until after Her Majesty had expired. That must have been almost too hard to bear.'

'It was at the time. But it could not be helped. Of course, air services have since improved out of sight. We lengthened the runway here to eleven thousand feet so that we can take jumbo jets after we open the terminal building this year.'

'Where will they be coming from?'

'Oh, all round: America, Australia, New Zealand. We will be operating a DC8 ourselves twice a week to New Zealand and Australia; twice to Honolulu, cargo to Los Angeles. Royal Tongan Airlines. The planes are already chartered and are sitting on the tarmac in Miami. All American crews, because we have an American operator as a partner. The big advantage of this is that when our flight arrives in Pago Pago, it becomes an American domestic flight, so it can pick up passengers from Honolulu and Los Angeles. When it gets back to Western Samoa, it becomes a Tongan flight again.'

'If I ask you to think back, what would you say is the most significant achievement – *your* most significant achievement perhaps – for Tonga in your lifetime?'

'Well, I did, of course, many things. I opened high schools, broadcasting, improved local shipping services, started the internal airline and now three television stations – one here, one in Ha'apai and one in Vava'u – to be run by an American-based Christian company. They will be licensed and we don't have to put up any money.'

'What has given you most pleasure over the period of your reign?'

'Everything is pleasant and constructive, but I think that television will be a big step because we can do school programmes in the daytime and probably transmit debates mostly in the evenings.'

'And the counterpart of that: what do you recollect as your most painful experience?'

'We lost a fishing boat once between Vava'u and Pago Pago. That was my most painful experience.'

'And with loss of life?'

'The whole boat. It went into a hurricane when we had no proper system of hurricane warnings. So we couldn't warn the boat. But now we have a twenty-four-hour watch. We can inform all craft. And we have not lost a boat since. Tupouto'a is going to Perth to accept a patrol vessel equipped with special instruments for marine surveys. Much of Tonga has not been surveyed in great detail. 'Eua and the two Niuas and islands in Ha'apai have never been properly surveyed. So we will be able to do all that too.'

'When you became King, you were perceived as an innovator. You were always questioning and thinking how you could change things for the better. You were an energiser of people, it seemed to me. How do you see yourself now?'

'Similar; but as I am no longer Prime Minister I can concentrate on questions of real significance and put aside the routine things. This is one of my schemes; look at that.' The King pointed to a model on a shelf. 'That is a mobile food kitchen: two cooks, plus four stoves to provide food for two hundred and fifty people in two hours. They are made in Germany for their army. We are buying one and the German army is donating another one. We are getting both to Tonga and are training six cooks; three are going to Germany on a finishing course and three are going to Hawaii to be taught how to operate an American fast-food truck. That will also be purchased to operate together with the two trailers. Our new sports stadium is large but there is no food. Somebody has to supply the food so that the people can go there after breakfast and stay all day. We will be able to feed the football crowds at Teufaiva: school football all day Friday, Rugby on Saturdays and throughout the season. This is a charity. All the profits will go into a hurricane relief fund. So in case of hurricane disasters, we will have lots of money.'

'Where will the food come from?'

'From New Zealand. Hamburger patties and hot dog sausages. Even hot dog buns from New Zealand bakeries. We will fly them to Tonga. We will also get a refrigerator truck for supplies of soft drinks.'

'Who will organise all this?'

'It will be operated by all the cooks who come from the police. They have a police accountant who will work out the cost. The police are right next door to the stadium. But we can also cook lunches and dinners for VIPs so that we can have Government dinners and lunches at our conference centre seminars and forums.'

My mind boggled at all this energetic but financially uncertain enthusiasm.

'Nobody is doing it, so now I am. It will also be filling the coffers of our charities. I get nothing out of it, but the people will be fed. We can go round the office blocks and shops at lunch time. The trailer is the best in Europe. They supply the German armed forces and NATO.'

'So it is well tested?'

'Oh yes. In the snows of Norway. When I went to the factory in Germany, there were thirty-six lined up, waiting to be airlifted to feed the Saudi Arabian armed forces. All climates and types of food.'

'So in a few months from now,' I said, 'in accordance with custom, you will be brought the first meal produced by the kitchens?'

'Of course,' the King replied, with anticipatory relish. 'There is another thing. We are negotiating with a Danish company to bring out portable dairy factories in forty-foot containers. When they are put on a concrete base, we will have the factory. They will take in all available supplies and produce homogenised milk, yoghurt, ice-cream and cheese. I'm hoping there will be enough milk so that we can have milk shakes in our mobile kitchens!'

'You have become a food entrepreneur, a food provider.'

'I am prepared to do anything: get into food, get into oil, get into anything.' The King laughed again.

'Would you say then that the monarchy has become increasingly active in a commercial sense?'

'Well, you see, in the past whenever we had disasters we had to look for funds to rebuild houses, feed the people, and so on. So I have always thought it was a good idea to let funds like that accumulate when there are no hurricanes. Then when the hurricanes hit we will have the capability of doing something. Hunger in a land of plenty can be a serious problem after a hurricane. So instead of asking the people to contribute to hurricane relief we will just ask them to eat and drink and we will store the profit. We will advertise all this on television. It is all going to come together at the same time.' The conviction was complete.

'Notwithstanding all your enthusiasms, there are some who have deep concern about what they see as the commercialisation of the monarchy: the generating of money and profit. Do you see any conflict or inconsistency between the traditional place – the constitutional place – of a monarch whose person is sacred and one who is the innovatory entrepreneur we have talked about?'

'Actually, I have all the ideas and I see exactly how they are going to work and then I hand them over to somebody else to put into practice. In this food business, it is the Minister of Police.'

I pondered these extra-portfolio potential responsibilities of a police minister.

'Part of the problem, I suspect, is that you carry with you for the first and only time, the highest customary ranking in Tongan history. Therefore you are still held in awe by large sections of the population. That person coming into business, into commerce . . .'

'I don't come into business. The Minister of Police does. I put the ideas into his head.'

'And so far as the kitchens are concerned, that is the police too?'

'That's right. The six cooks are all policemen.'

'I would like to turn now to another question. We have talked about the number of physical changes you have stimulated or presided over. In respect of the constitutional and political pressures that there are, some people today appear to think of you as having become more and more conservative. Is that right, would you say, or is that a public perception which you do not accept?'

'Well, let us say I am not a radical. In fact, I believe in evolution rather than revolution.'

'Of course. What sort of evolution then would you like to see or be willing to entertain in the latter years of your reign?'

'I think the old Constitution envisaged that the popular representatives would be elected – and they have been – without opposition. What is going to happen now is that a political party is being organised by sections of the population who have moderate views and who do not particularly like the popular representatives we have now. They are starting with a petition, a counter-petition to what the popular representatives have presented and with a gigantic procession numbering tens of thousands with four brass bands. The people are signing this petition in Niuatoputapu, Vava'u and Ha'apai as well as Tongatapu and 'Eua. That will be the beginning of a new political party.'

'What will its objectives be, do you think?'

'Instead of trying to make the present Government members of the Legislative Assembly a minority by inflating the popular representation, they want to use what is already there. They are hoping that the Ministers and the Representatives of Nobles will become members of the new party, so that it will begin with a parliamentary majority of its own. It will seek to elect members to displace some of the present popular representatives and then they will all work together to achieve full employment and care of workers, like making working conditions better, seeing that they are insured against injury and the like and liaising with workers outside Tonga so that they can be brought back and employed in our developing industries here.'

'Would I be right in thinking that this proposed political party – the first in Tonga – would be in essence a conservative party?'

'Well, it is proposed that it should be called the Christian Democratic Workers of Tonga.'

'That brings just about everybody in, doesn't it?'

'Yes, that's right; and because it is a Christian party they can use the Christian terms because they are there in their capacity as Christians.'

'Is it associated with any particular Church?'

'No, but it should draw all people who believe in Christianity and all workers and all people who have democratic inclinations.'

'Is it something that you would encourage, that you feel sympathetic towards?'

'Oh yes.'

'Basically, their objective is to support the monarchy, I assume?'

'Well they will support the Government and seek to influence it, particularly the Minister of Labour, to do things that will increase employment and take better care of working conditions. As I have said.'

'Do you envisage any changes in the *Fale Alea* in your lifetime?'

'That could happen, but in conditions of mutual confidence instead of confrontation. Confrontation will not achieve anything, but co-operation will.'

'Views seem to vary as to whether ministers should be from an elected base or continue to be appointed by you in your sole discretion.'

'Yes, well, in a parliamentary system like Westminster, the Sovereign appoints only the Prime Minister. Then the Prime Minister appoints all the ministers; but here I appoint everybody, from top to bottom. In a party system, there must be a party behind the Prime Minister. What these people here are trying to do is to create a party behind the Prime Minister that would be wide enough to get the allegiance of the majority of the people.'

'Do you think there is any real distinction between the perceptions of these matters in Tongatapu, particularly Nuku'alofa on the one hand; and Ha'apai, Vava'u, 'Eua and the Niuas on the other?'

'There might be some, although it is very difficult to get feed-back unless you go to every little *kava* party, but we hope to use the television stations to talk to them.'

'And you would want to see and encourage open debate on all subjects, irrespective of the views expressed?'

'Of course. It is always a good idea to know what people think, because if they think wrong ideas you can correct them. But you cannot do that if you don't know.'

'Traditionally of course you didn't know, because the *fono* was a gathering in which the people came to obtain or to hear the instructions that were to be given them by their noble; but your suggestion for open debate on television about the affairs of the people – education, health care, workers' conditions – will be a significant change for Tonga: the public discussion of these things. It already exists in the press to some extent but that is limited . . .'

'Our newspapers come out only once a week, but television comes every day, so you are right up to the minute.'

'Would an increase in the representation of the people be something that you would support?'

'Well there are now nine Representatives of the Nobles and nine Representatives of the People, instead of seven and seven as in the past. It is like a garnet; you have to strip off little pieces and add on little pieces. Much like a house.'

'But are you sympathetic towards the idea of increased numbers of elected representatives?'

'Under conditions where people are organised into a political party, particularly a comprehensive political party, then that sort of thing can be considered.'

'If you were able to gaze into your crystal ball to the year 2000, what sort of Tonga will we find?'

'If we get this refinery up and operating, our annual income will be something like a hundred million US dollars. We will put that aside for development, so we will have no trouble about funding it.'

'So you see a vastly improved Tonga, derived from this one project?'

'Oh, yes. The benefits of money will be freely available throughout the whole of the population. As the new factories come on stream, they will absorb more of our people in light industries. And, of course, we will also be starting major industrial development in Vava'u.'

'Can I turn now to the role of the Kingdom of Tonga in the region. It seems to me that the South Pacific has become an increasingly unstable part of the world and that the Pacific is no longer pacific in the sense that we originally understood it.'

'This is because there are problems that have not been thought about enough in the past. Fiji, of course, always had the Indian problem and they are reacting to that now. I think they should have reacted long ago but they did not do so. Papua New Guinea has an extraordinarily high crime rate; not only that, but thousands of their people have been infected with Aids.'

'Amid such problems – and there are plenty of others – do you

still see Tonga as the stable rock around which the Pacific waters
wash?'

'I believe so. When we get this oil refinery and the industries in
place, it will be an even firmer rock than it was.' The King roared
with laughter. 'It will have more secure foundations, you could say.'

'That touches on an interesting point, doesn't it, because we all
know that politics and economics are closely related?'

'Two sides of the same coin.'

'And one way to ensure that you have a quiet or quiescent political
life is to have a sound and developing economic life?'

'That is right.'

'Politics do not become so important then. But if you have want
and uncertainty . . .'

'Like Bangladesh . . .'

'Yes, then you will have fertile ground for political manoeuvre
and manipulation. Would you say therefore that given the economic
plans that you have fostered over the years, in all of them you have
had in the back of your mind that they do something, if successful,
towards keeping the political scene stable and quiet?'

'Oh yes. And of course social services like free education and
medicine and so on have to be paid for, and if they are to be improved
they have to be funded with more money. From somewhere.'

'How do you see the role of the Church – Church and State – in
all this?'

'The Churches have made a big contribution to education, but
except for the Mormons, they are financially handicapped. So they
all have problems.'

'And the Mormon Church is coming up for a big anniversary in
July this year: the centenary of the arrival of its first missionaries in
Tonga.'

'Yes, they will all be flying here in our plane, from Hawaii and
from New Zealand.'

'Do you think that Tonga has benefited from the Mormon
presence?'

'I think so. They teach people not to drink or smoke. That is
very good. Drinking is already producing a lot of accidents. We are
considering making liquor and tobacco state monopolies, so that the
profits from products which are essentially harmful will not go into
private hands, but will go to a socially constructive purpose such as
a sports fund to train and send athletes and sports-people to the
South Pacific Games, and so on. This is under study now. I am very
interested in sport and physical fitness, of course. We already have

a sports stadium at 'Atele that was funded by Taiwan. I want to acquire a comprehensive set of exercise equipment for it. Later on we will build other halls and equip them in Ha'apai and Vava'u. We are doing so well in rowing because we have bought special equipment for exercising rowers properly.'

'You have always seen sport as a very important part of Tongan society.'

'Yes, it teaches discipline and channels the energy of young people in the right direction.'

It was time for me to leave. Ninety minutes had elapsed. But it seemed right for me to say what I intended to try to do.

'I am going to make an attempt, no doubt flawed, to understand and portray what I have called "the New Friendly Islanders". So I have been talking over recent weeks to people from differing walks of life in differing circumstances; and listening to what they have told me, which is not necessarily what they tell others. So there will, I hope, be a spectrum of views and perceptions: some positive, some negative, some critical, some adulatory. But all, it has seemed to me, are concerned for Tonga. The Kingdom is at a singularly interesting stage in its history. I am going to start with my introduction to it in the 1950s; then, after so long an absence, come forward to today. I shall, in an impossibly short time, be trying, I suppose, to see how the past relates to the present and what that crystal ball may have in store. It will be neither a social survey nor an anthropological study, but it may offer a little external insight into the Tonga that approaches the twenty-first century. I wanted to end my questions and my listening with Your Majesty, so that there is some record of how *you* see things, to set beside my accounts of how some others perceive you, the Government, the Legislative Assembly and Tongan society today.'

The ADC saw me safely beyond the Palace gates. I was glad to have all that off my chest. The ever-faithful PM25 was waiting. So was Papiloa, who gave me a wooden Tongan piglet as 'a good luck charm'. It was a nice piece of Polynesian subtlety.

Next day I flew to Auckland, Sydney, Canberra and then back to England. It was early April. The daffodils were in full bloom and the spring blossoms were bursting forth. The grass was thick with lush new growth. The birds sang. I sat shirtless in the garden under a benign sun and wrestled with the tape recording of my conversation with the King.

A week later it was snowing again. 'Eseta would be pleased, I thought. I put on my heaviest winter suit and set off on the commuter trail to the Royal Institute of Public Administration in Regent's Park. Rush hour in a British Rail mainline station and the Underground escalators were once again the ultimate urban insanity, for me and countless other commuters. Tonga seemed moon miles away. Yet it was ever-present. The contrasts – and the daily uncertainties – said something about the realities of human life wherever it is lived.

I was going to need that little pig.

33

That Elusive Vision

So, one hundred years on, maybe we should look again at Basil Thomson's refusal to treat seriously that 'fatal experiment of engrafting Western customs upon their own ancient and admirable polity' and 'the sense of grotesqueness with which their present hybrid institutions inspire the best of them'. If he regarded the experiment as fatal then why, you may well ask, did he decline to treat it seriously?

It is at least arguable today that the supposed experiment, far from being fatal, helped to provide the foundations for the survival of a vulnerable island kingdom in a predatory colonial world, and that the importation and adoption of much that was untypically Tongan went some way towards establishing the integrity and distinctiveness of Tonga in the South Pacific – rather than the opposite – in the perceptions of the outside world. This period of transitional adjustment was brought to an end by Queen Salote's wish to return to customary ways and to abandon the imported vestmental frock coat and butterfly collar for the *ta'ovala* and *kafa*.

Perhaps it is Basil Thomson and not the Tongans who looks outmoded now or just plain wrong. It is not his fault, though. Life has moved on, that is all. It could not be assumed that the nineteenth-century Tongan way of life would last, irrespective of outside influences and internal needs. One hundred years later, the realities are starkly different in the computerised commercialism of Polynesian power.

The changes introduced by the 1875 Constitution must have been just as much of a shock to the system then as anything needed now. Tongans have *not* always been the same; the old missionaries knew that. It is a delusion to think that successive generations cannot absorb change without destruction of the key essentials of their society and traditions. To assume otherwise is a capitulation to vested interests in the land.

Today, the 'hybrid institutions' as represented by that nineteenth-century Constitution are under attack, yet survive. Structurally, that is. But the structure is creaking a bit, and is in need of engineering survey and repair.

The role and attitude of some of the thirty-three appointed nobles scarcely meet popular expectations of leadership by example in the modern world; while the lack of adequate public accountability, notably in respect of the Legislative Assembly and the Cabinet, is eating away confidence in the institutions of the Government and those who, from the top downwards, sustain them. Indeed, as 'Akalisi Pohiva has tried to demonstrate in his broadsheet *Kele'a*, the management of public money is just as dismal today as it was a century ago, although the sums now are substantially larger. So too is the cupidity. For the stakes in the 1990s could be high, not least if commercially exploitable oil is indicated.

There are prophets of doom and gloom in Tonga today, but then there always were. Some of them have been found, at one time or another, in the Nuku'alofa Club. My first was a German copra planter: 'The Tongan is not what he used to be. He's become soft on white bread, corned beef and Australian gin. None of the young people of today really know the customs and traditions of the past. Cotton-wool Tongans, that's what they are now, living in half-pie wooden houses and grown fat and bone idle . . .'

Our conversation was in 1954. Then, in March 1991, from a descendant of another German settler family: '. . . Tonga is going down. There is no doubt about it. No one remembers us now. The young people don't care about the past. All they are concerned with is a quick buck, videos and the disco. No, I don't like the prospects for the next century, even though I still want to see the year 2000 . . .'

In between, timewise, but in similar vein, was the late Dr 'Alokihakau 'Eva, the Kingdom's first and widely respected surgeon: 'The trouble with us Tongans is that we have given up the backbone for the wishbone.'

For 'Alo, Carl Riechelmann told me, the backbone was the tenets and times of Queen Salote; the wishbone, overseas aid. He too was speaking in the Nuku'alofa Club.

Attitudinal wringing of hands may be unavoidable in a changing and complex world, but it is ultimately self-defeating. Life is as it is, not how it should or might or could be, if only . . . The first reality is that life is unfair – in the beginning for the poor and the deprived; and in the end, unlikely as it may seem, for the privileged. It is an illusion to believe how much better it once was and thus how it should continue to be, not least because successive generations want change and create change before our eyes, which we must learn to recognise and accept.

It is no longer the meek who inherit the earth. Change may come about dramatically by revolt or insurrection, devastating or eliminating what went before like the French monarchy, the Czars of Russia or the Shah of Persia; or it comes about by evolution not revolution, as the King of Tonga would accept, thus changing the face without wrecking the body, building on what exists without destroying the institutional edifice.

Two things are needed to take Tonga, sociologically intact, into the twenty-first century. The first is a fundamental change of attitude to privileged status within a crucial section of Tongan society. The second is reform of the structures and tools of government, however created and to whomsoever responsible. The second is dependent upon the first. The one does not necessarily follow the other, but is the pre-empting basis for it.

The key is not the monarchy, but the nobles as perhaps was always the case. The instinct for self-perpetuation is not confined to an anachronistically feudal Tonga. The ingredients are essentially the same world-wide, in the past and in the present. Our history is full of examples of 'the people' rising against an oligarchic landed aristocracy. Politics determined such a rising in India, with the nationalisation of princely states and land. Religion determined another: in Iran with the emergence of powerful fundamentalism. Look back to the French, Russian and Spanish revolutions and those of Haiti; and for quite different reasons, to the slow sustained struggle against the bastions of apartheid in South Africa. Mercifully, the world is or has just been in a period of great movements for popular freedom and reform. Should Tonga seek to stay immune from its heady forward march?

There is, of course, another side to the debate, which is roughly that some of those in high places – not all – appear to condone, perhaps encourage, corruption and preferment; this plus nepotism, they contend, is essential to the survival in a modern world of the Tongan way of life or their view of it. They cite the burden of custom in a twentieth-century business economy. Yet it is they who want to continue to bear it. To do so, they argue, they need money. So inflated allowances and doctored claims are, as one person put to me, 'essential to enhance my income so that I can continue to comply with custom and its obligations'.

That argument is, of course, bogus. It assumes that custom is unchanging, that public tolerance will last for ever and that the rights, privileges and status of a landed aristocracy are immutable for all time in a pattern determined in a far-off era. If, as Futa Helu contends, money – not land – has become pre-eminent in Tonga, it is just possible, is it not, that the two may yet come together in the commercial prostitution of a great heritage.

The Tongans have astutely preserved themselves and their soil from foreign acquisitiveness and exploitation throughout the nineteenth and twentieth centuries. Can they resist the blandishments of 'the most dollar' as they enter and contemplate their future in the twenty-first?

Place your bets, ladies and gentlemen. We shall, in due course, find out.

There are ethical considerations and acceptable standards in public life that cross the boundaries of culture, language, race, religion and nationality: they are universal and, hopefully, impregnable, in Tonga and beyond. They reflect the selfless courage and endurance of Maui-'Atalanga and Maui Kisikisi in those uncluttered mythological days. That is what is needed now to enhance the prospects for the future together with the core riches of a proud Polynesian heritage.

For survival, intact, there is an even chance. The outcome will ultimately rest upon the wisdom and responsiveness of the leaders and the extent to which they are disposed, like Lavaka, to listen to the voices of their people. For if they do not, there may not be many who are left to begin listening by the year 2000 and thereafter. By then it could be too late.

The initiative has to be taken, very soon, by the King and his Ministers. Otherwise it could be wrested from them. With the introduction of television and the King's encouragement of public debate, the way should be open for the first time in Tongan history for unfettered discussion of social and political issues, unless the posturing protectionism of self-interest blocks the way.

The procedural suggestion from Deputy Prime Minister Langi Kavaliku for a royal commission to look at the Constitution and thus the possibility of a future fully elected parliament seems to me to be an eminently sensible and reasonable first step. It would enable the voice of the people – nobles and commoners alike – to be properly heard and analysed for the first time. Sales of *kava* should soar.

The voters of Tonga are not inexperienced or irresponsible. They are entitled to a central government chosen by means of a free and fair electoral process, a government which is accountable to them. So too they should be empowered to vote out of office a government or its ministers that they are discontented with or which is perceived to indulge in abuse of office. Unaccountable authoritarianism, however benevolent *in intent*, should be shown the exit notice. The learning experience from the new democracies of 1990, whatever the headaches from the wine of freedom, is that government without the electoral consent of the people is as inefficient as it is oppressive.

Evolution, not revolution . . . A lead should be given and may yet be given. Indeed, in this intriguing, complex and unique South Pacific island kingdom, there could be a lesson both for itself and for the wider world: that power voluntarily relinquished is respect, influence and thus stability, retained.

That is the elusive vision I have – for the New Friendly Islanders.

There will be many who seek to set the course of Tonga on its journey in the twenty-first century. The way ahead for them may well have difficulties as testing as those faced by Maui Kisikisi and Maui 'Atalanga.

How they fare we shall come to know only when the future unveils its secrets.

'When elephants fight, the grass gets trampled on.'
. . . An African saying

Epilogue

Into Space

There is in London a royal press release known as the Court Circular. It is issued from Buckingham Palace and appears in dignified prominence in the quality British press.

The first item is always the diplomatic comings and goings at Buckingham Palace as Heads of Mission present their credentials to, or take their leave of, the British Head of State. On Friday 10 July 1992 this appeared:

BUCKINGHAM PALACE
9 July: His Excellency Mr Sione Kité was received in audience by The Queen and presented the Letters of Recall of his predecessor and his own Letters of Commission as High Commissioner for Tonga in London.

His Excellency was accompanied by the following members of the High Commission:

Mrs Mele Takapautolo (Counsellor), Miss Kaimana Aleamotu'a (First Secretary) and Mr Tevita Vaipuna (Third Secretary).

Mrs Kité was also received by Her Majesty.

Sir David Gillmore (Permanent Under-Secretary of State for Foreign and Commonwealth Affairs) was present and the Household-in-Waiting were in attendance.

In those stylised words lay formal notification of the departure from London of the former High Commissioner for Tonga and recognition of the arrival and acceptance in post of his accredited successor.

The new High Commissioner is a commoner and no stranger to London. After a first degree and diploma at the University of New South Wales, he completed a Master's degree in the mid-1970s at London University's Institute of Commonwealth Studies. A chunky puckish man of shrewd intellect, he sports a neat goatee beard. Prior to his present appointment he was Deputy Chief Secretary and Deputy Secretary to the Cabinet in the Prime Minister's office in Nuku'alofa. I called on him at the High Commission offices at 36 Molyneux Street near Edgware Road.

'How's the book?' he asked. I never know how to answer that question, except in monosyllables. We talked a little and then he said, 'I suppose you've got all you want about Tonga's space satellite?'

'Tonga's what?'

He laughed. 'I am sure you heard me. Tonga's satellite. Didn't you mention it when you saw the King?'

'No. How could I? I didn't know about it. And he didn't refer to it. So are you telling me that the Kingdom of Tonga is to launch its own satellite into space?'

'Yes, I am. And before I came to London, I was directed by His Majesty to work on it on behalf of the Government.'

All I could manage was, 'Good God. That seems to raise a considerable number of questions.'

He smiled, not at all put out. 'Your scepticism is understandable,' he said indulgently. 'Like you, I too was sceptical at the beginning, and so were the Big Boys. Not any more though. Let me fill you in.'

It all seems to have begun in 1987 when Dr Matt Nilson retired from Intelsat (the largest and oldest operator of global satellite systems) to form the Nilson Research Corporation in San Diego. With the support of the King, Dr Nilson established a private company in Tonga with the principal object of promoting the Kingdom's telecommunications development. The company is called The Friendly Islands Satellite Communications Limited (Tongasat) with Princess Pilolevu Tuita as its titular head. Matt Nilson is managing director.

'The most precious asset in the satellite industry,' says Sione Kité, 'is the acquisition and "ownership" of orbital slots to house or accommodate satellites. They are allocated to sovereign states only – not to companies or commercial organisations – by the International Frequency Registration Board [IFRB]. This is a regulatory body within the auspices of the International Telecommunications Union [ITU] in Geneva.'

With the assistance of Tongasat, the Government of Tonga identified orbital slots not yet acquired by another sovereign state and submitted applications for these slots.

The initial reaction within the IFRB was one of disbelief that David should try to take on Goliath. 'They didn't claim that we had no right to apply,' says Sione Kité. 'All they doubted was our capability. The negotiations were long, hard and tough. But we were not deterred by the opposition to our application and after some four years the Board finally granted to Tonga the six orbital slots it had applied for.'

The system – to be called the Asia/Pacific Communications Network – will be centred on Tonga and will circle the equator about 250 miles into space. It will beam east to Hawaii, west to Europe, and to the North and South Poles.

In late 1991, Tongasat signed an agreement with the Unicom Satellite Corporation in Colorado to finance, build and launch Tonga's first satellite in 1993. The arrangements between the two companies were formally endorsed by the Government of Tonga; and work is now in progress for the launching of the satellite, probably from Cape Canaveral. It is likely to cost US$150–200 million, including site preparation and monitoring arrangements in the United States and Tonga.

'So what,' I asked the High Commissioner, 'do other South Pacific island governments think of this extraordinary venture by Tonga?'

His reply came without hesitation. 'They are all curious – with more than a hint of jealousy by some.'

So the Kingdom of Tonga is to launch and to possess this remarkable twenty-first-century version of its 'flying canoe'. At least there will be no problem with the Tonganisation of the English word. It will just be 'sa–ta–lie–tee'. And no glottal stops.

ACKNOWLEDGMENTS

Acknowledgments

My primary thanks are due to His Majesty King Taufaʻahau Tupou IV who condoned – indeed, sanctioned – my reappearance in his Kingdom to research and question on this third occasion.

With no little proprietary trepidation, I submitted the near-complete first-draft script to His Majesty who read through it during a week's visit to Britain in late November 1991. He pointed to a few aberrations in Tongan spelling, but made no suggestions for change to the text. The King wrote the Foreword to *The Friendly Islanders* in 1966. That was a very different book about a very different Tonga. I am deeply grateful for his magnanimity of response to my present reflections on his vastly changed island kingdom and people. His Majesty's consent to providing the Foreword to this book and his endorsement of its publication is evidence of a tolerance and open-mindedness not always perceived by his people.

My special thanks go to Her Majesty Queen Halaevalu Mataʻaho for selecting the royal *tapa* of Queen Salote which graces the cover and permitting its exclusive use for this purpose.

His Royal Highness Crown Prince Tupoutoʻa thoughtfully provided me with a car and driver throughout my time in Tonga in early 1991. Without the car, I would have dissolved defeated in the face of summer seasonal heat, humidity, and erratic taxis and telephones. Her Royal Highness Princess Salote Pilolevu was generous in her assistance in both London and Tonga. So indeed was her husband, Siosaia Maʻulupekotofa Tuita, High Commissioner for Tonga in London for much of the period concerned; and his successor, Sione Kité, whose experienced hand may well be missed in the organisation of the massive celebrations which will mark the seventy-fifth birthday of the King on 4 July 1993.

All the Ministers of the Crown on whom I called were gracious in their welcome both to me and to the outline of my intentions as described to them. None sought to influence my thinking in any way. To one, Dr Langi Kavaliku, I am particularly indebted. In his absence on leave, he allowed his private secretary, Leipua-ʻo-Fatafehi Palu, to assist in transcribing my first-draft words. She did so throughout my stay with good humour, unflagging courtesy and perseverance. Working in a second language, Leipua had to come to

terms with the technological mysteries and occasional misdemean-
ours of her new computer–word processor and to cope with dis-
rupting family and personal illnesses. Not once did she complain of
the obscurity or disorder of my hand-written pages.

Viela Ileini Tupou, private secretary to the royal Minister
for Foreign Affairs and Defence, was authorised to facilitate my
early movements and official appointments. She ensured that I kept
them by maintaining a watchful eye on the various drivers of PM25.
Without her persuasive charm, I might still have been floundering.
It was a delight to meet the mature woman I had known as a little
girl.

Masina Tu'i'onetoa was devotion to assigned duty personified, as
she steered me through the untimely onslaughts of March weather
in Vava'u.

I am grateful to all those with whom I was able to speak about
Tonga today and Tonga tomorrow. I was permitted to consume
more of their time than I had any right to expect, in some instances
on more than one occasion. Without them, my journey would have
been fruitless. Many spoke with an impassioned frankness that,
whatever their views, I found as compelling as it was unexpected. I
have sought to ensure that the observations they made to me in 1991
have been accurately recorded, whether attributed or not.

Pesi and Mary Fonua, founding father and mother of Vava'u Press,
gave me encouragement and practical help, not least with work on
the script when Leipua – or her miracle machine – were out of action
and they too, with their children, were temporarily afflicted by the
dreaded Tongan 'red eye' illness. It was a mark of their concern that
they were successful in not passing it on to me. They have kindly
permitted me to quote from their *Matangi Tonga*.

I must thank Pierre Encontre who provided me with shelter on
my arrival in Tonga; Earle Pangia Emberson on Pangaimotu Island;
Pat Matheson and Mikio Filitonga, against all odds, in Vava'u; and
Papiloa Foliaki and 'Ila at the Friendly Islander; the late Iona Papun-
gato'a Emberson Gluck, Christina Beetham, Felicia Holt and Cherie
Emberson Gluck at Sopu; and Nina and Sione Kinahoi. For his
welcoming hospitality and that of Kate, I am indebted to Carl
Riechelmann, President of the Nuku'alofa Club since 1975 and a
director of Royal Tongan Airlines. We had last worked together for
the Royal Visit to Tonga close to forty years earlier in December
1953. In Auckland, my thanks for hospitality and transport are due
to Beverley Baildon, Jennifer Reeves and Nan and Ken Greville; and
for the maverick ministrations of Graeme Baildon. In Canberra, I

was similarly welcomed by Satendra Nandan and Jyoti; and in Sydney, by Felix and Pat Emberson.

There are many others in Tonga who at different times and in various circumstances made my way easy when it could have been hard. That they did so with abundant enthusiasm albeit, on occasion, disarming uncertainty, made my re-entry into the heart of contemporary Polynesia so much more illuminating.

In England, I was once again beholden to Margaret who is also Fonu and who has spent a good part of her adult life married on my behalf to a shorthand notebook and editorial typewriter; Clare Walters, who applied the professional polish to the finished product within the miracles of a floppy disk; 'Akosita Fineanganofo, Deputy Secretary for Foreign Affairs, for timely reminders of some special features of Tongan spelling and pronunciation; 'Ofa Tu'i'onetoa, Private Secretary to the King and Tevita Kolokihakaufisi, Counsellor at the Tonga High Commission in London; Andrew Lawson for enlightenment about old Spanish; Celia Levett, my editor, whose clinical eye and polished skills rescued me from many an unwanted aberration or confusion; and for the assistance of Cable and Wireless plc.

Work on the script was begun in Sevenoaks in 1990. In Part One I have drawn on some material which appeared in *The Friendly Islanders*, 1967. The greater part of first-draft writing was done in Tonga between February and March 1991. It was continued in Sevenoaks, Chichester and London from April to June and completed a year later after the visit to London of the King and Queen. By the time of the twenty-fifth anniversary of their coronation on 4 July 1992, the spanking new Japanese-financed terminal building at Fua'amotu Airport had been in operation for a year.

Publication in 1993 has been made possible by the generous support of the Government of Tonga. This is virtually a repetition of what happened in respect of my first Tonga writing of forty years ago, and says much about the Kingdom, its Government today and the New Friendly Islanders. 'Sometimes the truth hurts a bit,' said 'Ofa Tu'i'onetoa, in a world-bridging telephone conversation with me, 'but that does not mean it is any less the truth.'

I can but hope so, for no one, other than myself, bears responsibility for the text.

Kenneth Bain

GLOSSARY

Glossary

'Aisi kilemi	Ice-cream
Eiki	Chief.
Éminence grise (Fr.)	An influential figure working behind the scenes in state policy.
En tout cas (Fr.)	All-weather.
Faifekau	Minister of the Church, preacher.
Faikava	Talking and drinking round the *kava* bowl.
Fale	Tongan house.
Fale Alea	Legislative Assembly.
Faute de mieux (Fr.)	For want of anyone or anything better.
Fiefia	Celebratory happiness or merry-making.
Fono	The traditional calling together of the people to hear the words of the chief or the Government.
Ha'amonga-a-Maui	'The Burden of Maui.' The ancient stone trilithon on Tongatapu.
Hou'eiki	The chiefs.
Kafa	A belt of coconut-fibre sinnet wrapped round the *ta'ovala*.
Kava	The social and ceremonial drink of the South Pacific. It is a solution of the pulp of the root of the *kava (piper methysticum)* plant mixed and strained in cold water. Drunk from half-coconut shells, it has a cleansing after-effect on the palate and is pleasantly thirst-quenching on a hot day. The Fijian word is *yaqona*.
Kelea	Conch shell. When blown in early days, the sound summoned the people to a *fono*.
Lakalaka	A rhythmical dance of celebration performed by men and women dancers in parallel lines.
Laupisi	Swelled-headed. Cheeky. Acting above your station.
Lento ma non gracioso (It.)	Slowly, but not gracefully.
Matai	Samoan family head.

Matapule	A lesser chief. Sometimes a spokesman.
Matangi Tonga	Literally 'Wind from Tonga'; a fair wind (from the south). A bi-monthly news magazine.
Ma'ulu'ulu	A sitting dance performed by either men or women.
Minisita Pa'anga	Minister of Finance.
Multum in parvo (Lat.)	Much in little.
Muu-muu	Colourful loosely-flowing ankle-length dress.
Nopeli	The Nobles.
'Osi	Finished.
Papalangi	A European. Originally, the strangers from over the horizon.
Pa'anga	Money. Tongan dollar.
Pola	The plaited stretchers of coconut fronds on which food is carried at a feast.
Raikoro (Fijian)	Village inspection. 'Safari.'
Sea	Chairman.
Sekelitali	Secretary. Often applied to the holder of the post of Chief Secretary of the Government.
Ta'ovala	A woven mat worn round the waist expressing humility in the presence of a person of higher rank.
Tapa	The beaten bark 'cloth' of the *hiapo* tree used for clothing, bedding, decoration and other ceremonial and domestic purposes. Designs are imprinted or stencilled by hand with earth dyes and dyes prepared from the sap of the *koka* and candlenut trees.
Tapu	Sacred or forbidden. It virtually combines both meanings.
Tau'olunga	A graceful dance for soloists or groups.
Tu'i Ha'atakalaua	A line of temporal kings. The holder of the title 'Tungi' is the sovereign head of this royal line.
Tu'i Kanokupolu	The line of temporal kings which emerged as paramount with the establishment of the Tupou dynasty. King Taufa'ahau Tupou IV is the twenty-second Tu'i Kanokupolu.
Tu'i Lau	The King of Lau; the title of the high chief of the eastern seaboard islands of Lau (a part of

	Fiji but with considerable Tongan influences and customs).
Tuʻi Tonga	The first dynasty to rule Tonga from about AD950 – literally, 'The Kings of Tonga'. They were spiritual as well as temporal rulers and as they represented the gods, they were regarded as sacred. The last Tuʻi Tonga became a Roman Catholic before he died in 1865, the only one of a long line to be a Christian.
Tukuʻaipe	Never mind. It doesn't matter.
ʻUmu	Food cooked in a Tongan earth oven, or the oven itself.
Vala	The ankle-length underskirt wrapped round the waist and legs.
Veni Vidi Vici (Lat.)	I came, I saw, I conquered (Julius Caesar in Britain, 47BC).

Tongan Orthography and Pronunciation

All words are constructed in a pattern of consonant-vowel-consonant-vowel. And the reverse.

Two consonants never come together, with only one exception: the letter 'g' is always preceded by an 'n', e.g. Tonga, Tungi, *ngaue* (work), *mohenga* (bed). Tonga used to be spelled Toga (as on early postage stamps) and the royal title Tungi was written Tugi. The contemporary *papalangi* pronunciation for Toga was often that of the Roman garment. This, plus the similar confusion abroad as to how to pronounce his own title of the time, caused the present King to require an 'n' to be added to both words.

Similarly in the Fijian language the name on the main international airport terminal building is spelt Nadi while being pronounced by all as Nandi.

Tonga is pronounced with a soft 'g', as in singer, not with a hard 'g', as in longer. The glottal stop before a vowel (or between vowels where it also separates the two sounds) indicates accentuation of the vowel which follows it. For example, 'Inoke (a first name) should have the emphasis on the first syllable, not the second. Nuku'alofa should be pronounced Nuku-ah-lofa, not with the stress on the penultimate syllable where it would usually fall.

Appendix
(see p. 134)

Viaje Politico – Cientifico
Alrededor del Mundo
por las Corbetas
Descubierta y Atrevida
Al Mando de los Capitanes de Navio
D. Alejandro Malaspina
y
Don José de Bustamante y Guerra
Desde 1789 a 1794
Capitulo V

Navegación de las corbetas desde el puerto Jackson hasta Islas de los Amigos. Escala en la Bahía Maurelle del Archipiélago de Vavao y reconocimientos interiores del mismo Archipiélago.

El Piloto Hurtado tuvo orden de enterrar en el sitio donde estaba el cuarto de circulo, una botella, la cual encerraba el papel auténtico de la llegada nuestra y de la posesión que habíamos tomado de todo el Archipiélago en nombre de Su Majestad con el consentimiento del mismo Vuna; y para que este acto solemne tuviese la mayor autenticidad así a la vista de los naturales como para noticia de los que nos siguiesen en aquellos mares, ya enterrada la botella se arbolaron en el mismo sitio las insignias, y las saludaron ante entrambas tripulaciones con siete veces de ¡Viva el Rey! y luégo los naturales, que estaban en la Descubierta, los cuales, a imitación de Vuna, hicieron igual número de aclamaciones.